Reinhold Pauli

Drei volkswirtschaftliche Denkschriften

aus der Zeit Heinrichs VIII. von England

Reinhold Pauli

Drei volkswirtschaftliche Denkschriften
aus der Zeit Heinrichs VIII. von England

ISBN/EAN: 9783743661653

Hergestellt in Europa, USA, Kanada, Australien, Japan

Cover: Foto ©Suzi / pixelio.de

Weitere Bücher finden Sie auf **www.hansebooks.com**

Drei
volkswirthschaftliche Denkschriften

aus der Zeit

Heinrichs VIII. von England.

Zum ersten Male herausgegeben

von

Reinhold Pauli.

Aus dem dreiundzwanzigsten Bande der Abhandlungen der Königlichen Gesellschaft
der Wissenschaften zu Göttingen.

Göttingen,
Dieterich'sche Verlags-Buchhandlung.
1878.

Drei volkswirthschaftliche Denkschriften aus der Zeit Heinrichs VIII. von England

zum ersten Mal herausgegeben

von

Reinhold Pauli.

Der Königl. Gesellsch. der Wissensch. vorgelegt am 4. Mai 1878.

Unter der grossen Masse der im Jahre 1540 beim Sturze Thomas Cromwells, Grafen von Essex, mit Beschlag belegten und heute im *Public Record Office* zu London aufbewahrten Papiere befinden sich ausser der Privatcorrespondenz, ausser diplomatischen und allen möglichen öffentlichen Actenstücken, wie sie jetzt nach und nach in Brewers gewaltigem Regestenwerke [1] verzeichnet werden, auch originale, bisher unbeachtet gebliebene Abhandlungen, die dem kühnen und mächtigen Staatsmanne in den Tagen der durch ihn zumal in England angebahnten Umwandlung zu verschiedenartigen Zwecken eingereicht wurden. Dass einige derselben sich eingehend mit den volkswirthschaftlichen Problemen des Tags befassen, wird nicht Wunder nehmen, seitdem aus der Geschichte der Nationalökonomik bekannt ist, wie sehr diese Fragen im Zeitalter der Reformation überall emporschiessen, und wie in England speciell während des sechszehnten Jahrhunderts bereits in lebhafter Discussion die deutlichen Vorläufer der grossen Periode der nationalen Volkswirthschaftslehre auftauchen.

Im Allgemeinen zeigen sie denselben Charakter, wie ihn Schmoller einst über die nationalökonomischen Ansichten in Deutschland während der Reformationsperiode aufgestellt hat [2]). Sie befassen sich von

---

1) Letters and Papers foreign and domestic of the reign of Henry VIII. by J. S. Brewer. Vol. IV. Part. III. 1876 erst bis 1530.

2) G. Schmoller, Zur Geschichte der nationalökonomischen Ansichten in

allen Seiten, aber freilich höchst ungleichartig, mit den mehr aufdämmernden, als klar gewordenen Principien, die dem allgemeinen Nutzen zu Grunde liegen, während zwei grosse Momente als Typus der Zeit und der noch vorwiegend scholastisch-klerikalen Autoren selber die Vorstellungen durchaus beherrschen. Auch in England nämlich richtet sich die religiös-moralische Anschauung so mächtig gegen den Andrang des Eigennutzes, dass der Staat als die allein rettende Kraft angerufen wird den jähen Umschwung in der Production der Güter zu hemmen und vor allen den Ackerbau gegenüber den entsittlichenden Wirkungen des Handels wieder in seine alten Vorrechte einzusetzen. Auch in England macht sich der aller Orten empfundene starke Druck der Preisveränderung geltend und soll die Gesetzgebung gegen das Eindringen neuer Betriebsformen und den monopolistischen Handelsverkehr eben so gut einschreiten wie gegen die in Folge des Zusammenbruchs eines alten Arbeitssystems in Brodlosigkeit und unbefriedigter Begier entfesselte Menge.

Viel mächtiger jedoch als alle materiellen oder geistlichen Reformideen wirkte in England die allgemeine sociale Revolution, die auf den hervorragenden Gebieten der Gütererzeugung im Grunde doch seit der Befestigung neuer politischer Zustände durch das Haus Tudor und jedenfalls lange vor der Zeit eingetreten war, ehe sich das Inselreich definitiv aus der Papstkirche los riss. An die Stelle des patriarchalischen Ackerbaus auf Grund des Dreifeldersystems trat die Speculation, die in der Feldgraswirthschaft, in umfassender Beseitigung der Bauernhöfe und deren Ersatz durch Zeitpacht ihren Vortheil fand. Statt der kleinen freien Landeigenthümer, die seit dem Statut Heinrichs VI. von 1430 nur bei einer Jahresrente von 40 Schilling das Wahlrecht und politische Rechte überhaupt bewahrten, kamen Grosspächter empor die zumal nach dem Ende der Thronkriege in längeren Contracten und mit völlig anderem Betrieb den grössten Theil von Grund und Boden bewirthschafte-

---

Deutschland während der Reformationsperiode in der Zeitschrift für die gesammte Staatswissenschaft XVI. 712. Tübingen 1860.

ten¹). Der neue Betrieb aber wurzelte in der Einhegung oft auch des Gemeindelands und in der massenhaften Verwandlung des Ackers in Schafweide, wodurch denn die ländliche Arbeitskraft meist ausgetrieben und brodlos wurde. Hatte der Untergang vieler Grossgrundherren während der Kriege eines Menschenalters und die berechtigte Strenge, mit welcher Heinrich VII. dem Wiedererstarken des Adelsstands entgegentrat, schon die Auflösung der alten feudalen Gefolgschaften, die denselben bisher im Felde wie auf seinen Schlössern umgaben, nach sich gezogen, so muste die unter Heinrich VIII., Anfangs allmälich, dann aber mit einem mächtigen Schlage vollzogene Aufhebung der Klöster, welche bis dahin ein Fünftel des Lands besessen und in ihrer Weise rationell bewirthschaftet hatten, eine noch grössere Menschenmenge unversorgt hinausstossen, so dass die niedere Bevölkerung durch die Lage von Handel und Gewerbe und bei der wesentlich auf Staatsmonopol begründeten Finanzwirthschaft der Zeit nun vollends in arges Gedränge gerieth²).

Auf dem Gebiet des Handels aber regten sich nicht minder das alte Wesen umstürzende Kräfte. Grosse privilegirte Corporationen hatten immer mehr den Verkehr in wenigen hervorragenden Emporien zusammengezogen, so dass die vielen Binnenstädte, überdies von den Umwandlungen im Ackerbau empfindlich getroffen, rasch verarmten. Im auswärtigen Verkehr, zumal auf den niederländischen Märkten wurde die bis dahin noch oft latente Speculation entfacht, das Creditwesen angebahnt, der Wechsel in die Masse der Werthzeichen des so lange starr liegenden Volkscapitals hineingeschoben. Wohl drehte sich der Umsatz zwischen Stadt und Land, zwischen Binnenland und Ausland nach wie vor um die seit den frühsten Zeiten viel begehrten nationalen Güter: Metalle, Leder, Wolle. Aber Dank der Arbeitstheilung suchten an Kauf und Verkauf, an Lagerung und Spedition, an Bearbeitung und Ausfuhr schon verschiedene andere Gruppen des Volks in Handel und

---

1) W. Stubbs, Constitutional History of England III, 551—554.
2) W. Roscher, Zur Geschichte der englischen Volkswirthschaftslehre, S. 9 (aus Band III der Abhandlungen der Königl. Sächsischen Gesellschaft der Wissenschaften). Leipzig 1851.

Handwerk zu verdienen und drinnen den Wettstreit mit dem Monopol, draussen mit dem mannigfach überlegenen Gewerbfleiss anderer Nationen aufzunehmen. Indess die niederen Schichten und der Mittelstand nicht nur, von allen Seiten bedrängt und in steigender Gährung, sondern auch der Staat, das Königthum im Rath und im Parlament, obwohl dasselbe in der Person Heinrichs VII. geradezu wie der erste Bankhalter des Landes erschienen war, empfanden doch die Noth der Zeit am heftigsten durch die Steigerung der Preise, die sich, was freilich Roscher so früh noch nicht wahr haben will[1]), auch in England schon fühlbar machte. Dass im Gelde der Reichthum stecke, dass das Geld im Lande zu halten, immermehr herein zu ziehen sei, war bereits auf allen Seiten das mercantilistische Glaubensbekenntniss. Ein stark protectionistischer Zug gegen die Fremde, längst vorhanden und seit dem fünfzehnten Jahrhundert in der Handelspolitik laut ausgesprochen[2]), gedieh zusehends

Alle diese Erscheinungen nun geben sich auch in den Aufsätzen kund, denen hier ihre Stelle angewiesen werden soll.

Der Zeit nach fallen sie ungefähr in die Mitte zwischen der *Utopia* des Sir Thomas More und einigen merkwürdigen, neuerdings aufmerksam beachteten literarischen Erzeugnissen aus der Epoche Heinrichs VIII. und Eduards VI. In ihrem geistigen Gehalt stehen sie beiden Endpuncten entschieden nach. Denn abgesehen von der treuen Bespiegelung der in Wirklichkeit bestehenden Verhältnisse bleibt doch die Utopia schon wegen des platonisch dichterischen Gewandes als Staatsroman, wegen ihrer socialistischen, ja, communistischen Abstractionen in alle Wege ein wunderbares Product des Menschengeistes. Wie in seinem Leben unvermittelt zwischen zwei Zeitalter gestellt, trug More auch als Autor ein Doppelgesicht. Während er jeden ausgelacht haben würde, der seine utopistischen Gebilde für bare Münze genommen hätte, blickte er gleichwohl angstvoll spähend in die Zukunft und witterte hinter dem

---
1) A. a. O. S. 14.
2) The Libell of Englishe Policye 1436, Text und metrische Uebersetzung von W. Hertzberg mit einer geschichtlichen Einleitung von R. Pauli, Leipzig 1878.

kräftigen Rechtsschutz, wie ihn Heinrich VIII. handhabte, mit Sicherheit bereits den despotischen Druck derselben Gesetze ¹). Der fromme Hugh Latimer dagegen, einst Bischof von Worcester und unter der blutigen Maria am 16. October 1555 zu Oxford auf dem Scheiterhaufen verbrannt, erinnert in seiner bäuerlichen Herkunft, in dem praktischen Blick für die Natur der Dinge, den er vom Vater geerbt, in Mutterwitz und volksthümlicher Beredsamkeit, in der warmen evangelischen Überzeugung wie kein anderer Engländer an den deutschen Luther. Auch er stand mitten in seinem Volk, dessen materielle Nothstände er klar durchschaute. Der treffende, gemeinverständliche Ausdruck, in welchem er die jedermann berührenden Zustände auf die Kanzel brachte, stand in schönem Ebenmass zu der Bildung, die er von den hohen Schulen zu Padua und Cambridge mitgebracht hatte ²). Neben ihm jedoch darf sein Zeitgenosse und Antipode Cardinal Reginald Pole nicht übersehen werden, der, selbst königlichen Geblüts, das eine mit Latimer gemein hatte, dass sie beide die wirthschaftlich so gewaltig eingreifende Aufhebung der Klöster in England erlebten, während, als More 1516 seine Utopia veröffentlichte, Cardinal Wolsey, der damals das Reich lenkte, noch nicht die Genehmigung des Papsts erwirkt hatte auch nur die kleinen grundverdorbenen monastischen Institute zu beseitigen. Wenn Pole, humanistisch und theologisch gelehrt, im Auslande der alten Kirche treu blieb und deshalb über die wirthschaftlichen Zustände der Heimath kaum Autorität sein konnte, so ist er doch gleichfalls von einem ihm von der Studienzeit in Padua her nahe verbundenen Landsmann als Charakterfigur in einem eigenthümlichen Dia-

---

1) Brewer zu Letters and Papers II, p. CCLXX. CCLXXII. Im Übrigen Roscher a. a. O. S. 6 und Wiskemann, Darstellung der in Deutschland zur Zeit der Reformation herrschenden nationalökonomischen Ansichten, S. 38 (Preisschrift gekrönt und herausgegeben von der Fürstlich Jablonowskischen Gesellschaft). Leipzig 1861.

2) Works of Hugh Latimer, Parker Society Edition, 2 Vols. Cambridge 1844. 1845, insonderheit die autobiographische Notiz in der Predigt vom 8. März 1549, I, 101 vgl. Roscher, a. a. O. S. 14.

log¹) verwendet worden um von seinem unprotestantischen, jedoch bekanntlich mittleren Standpunct aus eine Art Politik an dem pedantischen Bilde der Hauptkrankheitserscheinungen und ihrer Curen und im Einzelnen dieselben ökonomischen Fragen und zwar in derselben Richtung zu erörtern, wie sie ohne grosse Unterschiede bei More und bei Latimer begegnen.

Da bieten nun unsere Aufsätze ein lehrreiches Bindeglied. Sie sind gerichtet an den dunklen gewaltthätigen Emporkömmling, der in seiner Jugend die politische wie die Handelswelt in Italien und Flandern mit eigenen Augen kennen gelernt, unmittelbar aus dem Sturze Wolseys in der königlichen Gnade gedieh den kirchlichen Supremat Heinrichs VIII. aufrichtete und eben Hand anlegte, die grossen, im Reichthum erstickenden Klöster in Stücke zu zerschlagen. Sir Thomas More ist am 5. Juli 1535 auf Towerhill hingerichtet worden. Thomas Cromwell aber, der unter den Titeln eines Vicegerenten und Generalvicars als des Königs rechte Hand in Kirchensachen die durchgreifendsten Veränderungen traf, erschien bereits den Leuten, Freund und Feind, als allmächtiger Minister. Noch war Anna Boleyn Königin, noch waren die Launen des eigenwilligen Monarchen nicht entfesselt. Wer durfte zweifeln, dass Cromwell lange Jahre die volle Gunst, den weitesten Einfluss behaupten werde. Kein Wunder, wenn ihm verwandt gestimmte Geister, niederer Herkunft wie er, weder akademisch noch literarisch fein gebildet, die als Kleriker oder Laien mit der alten Kirche gebrochen hatten und dennoch die wirthschaftliche Lage Englands kaum mit anderen Augen ansahen als die bedeutendsten Landsleute vorher oder nachher, den Inhaber der Gewalt mit ihren Eingaben bestürmten. Gerade wegen ihrer unmittelbaren Auffassung, wegen der Besserungsvorschläge, die sie einfliessen lassen, wegen

---

1) England in the reign of King Henry the Eighth. a Dialogue between Cardinal Pole and Thomas Lupset, Lecturer in Rhetoric at Oxford, by Thomas Starkey, Chaplain of the King, ed. by J. M. Cowper. Early English Text Society, Extra Series N. XII. 1871. Briefe an Starkey, der 1535 bei Pole in Padua weilte und 1538 starb, sind abgedruckt von H. Ellis, Original Letters, Second Series II, 54. 70. 73. 76. 77.

der rohen, von unfertigem Protestantismus angehauchten Sprache gewinnen dieselben doppelte Bedeutung in einem Moment, als der König, kirchlich bereits Selbstherrscher, nun auch durch Spoliation des Klosterguts sein Regiment finanziell und wirthschaftlich unabhängig hinzustellen gedachte.

Ueber Ursprung, Zeitpunct, Gedankengang und Tendenz der drei Abhandlungen sei hier dem Text das Nöthige vorausgeschickt.

I. Ueber den Stapel und die Naturproducte Englands, obwohl ohne Namen und wegen des etc. am Ende anscheinend unvollendet, ist doch mit Bestimmtheit einem gewissen Clement Armstrong beizulegen, von dem sich gleichfalls in der Hinterlassenschaft Cromwells ein starker Band, betitelt: Clement Armstrongs Sermonen und Declarationen gegen papistische Ceremonien von derselben Hand, Orthographie und Argumentation, daher vermuthlich im Original vorgefunden hat. Eine Probe ist der Denkschrift unter I^a beigegeben, ingleichem unter I^b ein von derselben Hand absichtsvoll anonym geschriebener Brief, der nur an Cromwell gerichtet sein kann: Ein Brief an meinen Meister ich kann nicht sagen von wem. Der Name Armstrong, damals wie heute in Schottland verbreitet, begegnet oft genug in Acten und Briefen der Zeit, freilich nicht in Verbindung mit dem Vornamen Clement, so dass der Verfasser, auf den es ankommt, schwerlich eine amtliche Stellung einnahm. Dass er ein Geistlicher und zwar von protestantischer Richtung war, ist unschwer aus der Abhandlung wie aus den Sermonen zu entnehmen. Er zeigt sich aber nicht nur mit der Landesgeschichte und besonders der mercantilen vertraut, sondern steht mitten in den heftigen Reibungen der verschiedenen Gesellschaftsclassen. Er weiss in Calais und an den Handelsplätzen der Niederlande so gut Bescheid wie in London und hat sich eine bedeutende Waarenkunde, namentlich hinsichtlich der Wolle angeeignet. Die Preiserhöhung der Gewürze schreibt er den Portugiesen, der Schafe in Vliess und Fleisch der zusammengreifenden Speculation der Grundbesitzer und der Stapelkaufleute zu. Indess auch er selber, vom Speculationsgeist der Zeit ergriffen, hat sich in ein Holzgeschäft eingelassen. Sein Brief I^b, vermuthlich schon 1532 an Cromwell gerichtet, den er *my maister* nennt, führt

Beschwerde gegen einen Betrüger, der mit seinem Gelde durchgegangen. Er scheint sich überhaupt als Pamphletist mit den brennenden Tagesfragen in echt englischem, der Fremde abgeneigtem Sinn befasst zu haben. Weder die elegante Diction, noch der platonische Socialismus des Sir Thomas More ist bei ihm zu suchen. Er will die Stände und Classen auseinander, bei althergebrachtem Beruf und entsprechender Arbeit erhalten wissen und ereifert sich wie gegen das Eindringen fremder Waare so gegen das Monopol der Kaufmannschaft und die Leiden des Ackerbaus in Folge der Einhegungen. Stil und Satzbildung erscheinen mehr derb und kräftig als gelenk oder gar wohl gegliedert. Indess sind sie doch, ohne dass man weiter an der Rechtschreibung zu rühren als gelegentlich ein *v* statt *u* zu setzen braucht, leicht verständlich, wenn nur die endlosen Perioden durch moderne Interpunction eingetheilt werden. Einige chronologische Daten: p. 17 die Notiz, dass der Kaufmann Crosby vor 44 Jahren zuerst Handel nach Spanien getrieben habe, was das Jahr 1519 als Abfassungszeit ergeben würde, p. 17. 18 die Sehnsucht nach einem Handel und Völkerrecht überwachenden Kaiser, was an den Regierungsantritt Karls V. erinnern könnte, p. 38 das frische Gedächtniss der von den Londoner Lehrlingen am bösen Maitage 1517 verübten Excesse, könnten den Gedanken erwecken, als sei die Schrift wirklich um das Jahr 1519 entstanden, wenn der scharf unkatholische Ton und der Zusammenhang mit Cromwell nicht widersprächen. Vielleicht liegt in jenen Daten und in dem gänzlichen Mangel von Anspielungen auf die wechselvolle europäische Politik der Zeit und die mächtigen seit 1529 in England eingetretenen kirchenpolitischen Umwandlungen der Vorsatz die Persönlichkeit und die Beziehungen des Verfassers wirksam zu verschleiern. Jedenfalls berührt diese Abhandlung so wenig wie die beiden anderen die erste grosse elementare Gegenerschütterung, die im Herbst 1536 mit der Erhebung der nordenglischen Gemeinen, der sogenannten *Pilgrimage of grace*, wider die volkswirthschaftlichen und kirchlichen Neuerungen eintrat.

Der Gedankengang dieser Denkschrift Armstrongs, zugleich der umfangreichsten, ist nun folgender. In dem Jahrhundert von Richard II. bis Eduard IV. entsprach die Wollausfuhr durch den Stapel in Calais der Production und geschah gegen baares Geld. Seit Eduard IV. aber haben sich die Stapelkaufleute unmässig vermehrt. Während auf den flandrischen Märkten die Nachfrage und der Preis der englischen Wolle gleich rasch stiegen, begannen die Londoner fremde Waare statt Geld heim zu bringen. Gleichzeitig durch den übertriebenen Wollankauf verleitet, bezahlten die Niederländer nur einen Theil in Gold und wiesen das Uebrige auf die Märkte in Antwerpen, Bergen op Zoom und Middelburg an. Da das Pfund Sterling zu 28 Schilling Flemisch angenommen wurde, zogen die Stapler Wechsel auf die Corporation der Merchant Adventurers in London und verschifften bei dem auswärtigen Agio von 8 bis 12 Pfennig vom Pfund lieber fremde Waaren nach England. Eine andere Neuerung war die Wolle in Calais lagern zu lassen und beim Verkauf den Preis auf die Merchant Adventurers in London anzuweisen. Dadurch wurde der Einkauf flandrischen Tuchs zum grossen Schaden der königlichen Zölle abgeschnitten. Obwohl die Anweisungen mit den Siegeln der niederländischen Städte versehen wurden, gieng doch im Kriege von 1488 viel englisches Eigenthum zu Grunde, ehe König Heinrich VII. und sein Rath den Unfug erkannten. Zum grössten Verderben hat London seit 60 Jahren den Wollhandel der Landstädte vernichtet. Indem die Preise von den Wollmaklern gesteigert wurden, verwandelten Grundherren und Pächter durch Einhegungen Ackerland massenhaft in Schaftrift und zerstörten dadurch Ackerbau und Bauerstand. Da die Geistlichen vergassen, was Gottes Wort verbietet, gediehen Irrthum und Sünde. Alle populären Argumente richten sich gegen Gottes Anordnung, die den verschiedenen Ländern besondere Gaben zutheilt. Jetzt sucht ein Reich das andere zu berauben und, was doch die Sonne nicht zulässt, das fremde Gut zu pflanzen. Solche Unklugheit muss sich zumal in England rächen, wo seit 60 Jahren 400—500 Dörfer durch Einhegungen zerstört sind. Ein einziger Stapler in London hat das Verderben von 4000 bis 5000 Gemeinen, ein einziger Schafzüchter von 1000, 1200, 1400 Menschen auf dem Gewissen. Durch alle Experimente einer naturwidrigen Production aber wird die Wolle nicht feiner, sondern gröber. Da liegt auch die Ursache, weshalb England auf dem flandrischen Markt von Spanien, das rein englische Tuch von dem viel geringeren spanisch-englisch gemischten verdrängt wird. Nicht minder ist Schafffleisch als Nahrungsmittel schlechter und geringer geworden. An solcher Vernichtung der alten Art des Ackerbaues und der Viehzucht ist der Stapler Schuld, wie kein Dieb ohne Hehler ist. Ferner entziehen die Londoner Kaufleute dem englischen Handwerk die Arbeit, indem sie fremde Fabricate z. B. parfümierte Rosenkränze unter dem Vorwande einführen, dass sie in der Heimath nicht so billig herzustellen seien. So geht das Geld hinaus statt im Lande zwischen Bauern, Handwerkern und Grundherren umzulaufen. In London widmen sich seit 50 Jahren viel zu viel junge Leute der Kaufmannschaft, indem sie auf Stundung Tuch einkaufen um damit draussen zu speculieren, wodurch der alte ehrsame Handel genöthigt wurde die Ausfuhr aufzugeben und statt dessen mit dem Capital an der Börse Wucher zu treiben und als Adventurers die Wechselzahlung von hüben und drüben zu vermitteln. Als viele jener Anfänger faillierten, boten die Tuchmacher ihre Waaren den Osterlingen des Stahlhofs an, die sie früher nur von englischen Kaufleuten bezogen hatten. Jetzt kaufen auch die Osterlinge auf Stundung, während sie ehedem Massen von Gold und Silber ins Land brachten. Von zwei zu unterscheidenden Hansen, der preussischen und der der Hansestädte, ist jene vortheilhaft, weil sie noch baar zahlt, diese gefährlich, weil sie Ein- und Ausfuhr an sich reisst und die Geldcirculation hemmt. Während das arme Volk mit fremder, werthloser Waare überschwemmt wird, sind Gold und Silber, gemünzt und ungemünzt, immer seltener geworden. Es wäre unklug, die Fremden ganz auszusperren, aber das Gesetz sollte die eigenen Unterthanen vor Misshandlung schützen. Die grosse Schuld Londons kam durch den Mai 1517 an den Tag, als sich die arbeitslose Menge gegen die fremden Händler erhob, die alle Läden füllten. London aber ist nicht allein geschaffen um nur durch Handel und Umsatz reich zu werden und grenzenloser Unsittlichkeit zu fröhnen. Ein weiser Rathsherr sollte London reformieren, nicht etwa durch Gewalt, wie die Geistlichkeit fordert, die sich den Hass und Neid der Gemeinen erweckt hat. Vor Allem aber sollte wieder auf Baarzahlung bestanden und sollten Tuche nur aus reiner Wolle angefertigt werden, damit die Niederländer gehindert würden mit gemischter und gestreckter, als englisch ausgegebener Waare die Deutschen anzuführen. Alles Elend entspringt daraus, dass ein vom Gesetz geordneter Stapel fehlt.

II. Wie das Volk angeleitet werden kann ein Gemeinwohl aufzurichten scheint Bruchstück, das zwar auf der Mitte einer Seite, aber ohne einen angekündigten Gegenstand weiter auszuführen endet. Der Aufsatz ist von anderer Hand als I. und auch in anderem Stil geschrieben und zeigt anderweitiges Interesse, so dass man ihn, obschon dieselben Ideen anklingen und ähnliche Ziele verfolgt werden, schwerlich dem Clement Armstrong zuschreiben darf. Der anonyme Verfasser argumentiert folgendermasen: Wie der König nur in Uebereinstimmung mit dem göttlichen Gesetz gut regieren kann, so soll auch alle Obrigkeit und das Volk selber nur von den ihnen vom Schöpfer vorgezeichneten Gaben leben. Das Gemeinwohl wird einem mystischen Körper verglichen. Fremde Glieder wie der Advocat und Kaufmann, vor allen Bettelbruder, Mönch, Canonicus und andere kuttentragende Heuchler können ihm gefährlich werden. Alle wirklichen Glieder sind dazu da je nach Rang und Stand für das Gemeinwohl zu arbeiten. Nur wenn jedes für sich seinen Zweck erfüllt, haben alle zu leben statt zu betteln, zu rauben und zu morden. Der Verfasser verlangt daher auf dem Lande wieder den Ackerbau, in den Städten die Tuchmacherei aufzurichten. Durch königliche Commission soll in allen Grafschaften das brach liegende Land wieder zu Acker werden, der 30000 Pflüge und 100000 Menschen mehr beschäftigen könnte. Ebenso muss um nach alter Prophezeiung England in ein Paradies zu verwandeln das Handwerk in den Städten wieder Arbeit haben. Zu diesem Zweck ist durch Reichs- und Municipalgesetze strenger Schutzzoll einzuführen für alle solche Güter, die im Lande selber erzeugt werden, und mit Strafe einzuschreiten gegen einheimische und fremde Kaufleute, die das Land mit fremder Waare überschwemmen, solche ausgenommen, die in England schlechterdings nicht producirt werden kann und durch Vertrag geschützt ist. Die Ausnahmen sollen mit dem Londoner Handwerk verabredet werden. Wie viel Arbeitskraft liegt allein schon dadurch brach, dass die englische Wolle nicht einmal zur Hälfte im Inlande zu Tuch verwebt wird. Das

Reich kann sich sehr wohl durch Ackerbau und Gewerbe erhalten. Anknüpfend an einen Geheimrathsbeschluss, der vor zehn oder zwölf Wochen erlassen wurde, wird nun eingehend vom Bücherdruck gehandelt, der ebenfalls vom Auslande frei zu machen ist. Des Königs Licenz ist für jedes Werk, damals fast ausschliesslich Bibeln und Gebetbücher, erforderlich. Obwohl Tyndals Neues Testament, das 1526 im Auslande gedruckt wurde, viel Gutes gestiftet hat, ist es doch rathsam allen Druck selber zu besorgen und durch Verbot des fremden zu erzwingen. Dabei werden denn Privilegien gegen den Nachdruck erforderlich. Zucht und Ordnung aber kommen allen zu gut. Man soll auch die Bibel, was offenbar auf die von der Regierung bald zugelassene Uebersetzung des Miles Coverdale anspielt, nicht im Auslande drucken lassen. Ingleichem kann England eben so gut wie Frankreich sein eigenes Papier anfertigen, wozu zwei Papiermühlen hinreichen.

III. **Wie das Reich durch Arbeit und Wiederaufrichtung des Ackerbaus zu reformieren ist** zeigt von I. und II. verschiedene Hand und Orthographie und wäre einem dritten Verfasser zuzuschreiben, wenn nicht Stoff, Behandlungsweise und einzelne Formeln wie *In example* bestimmt an Armstrong erinnerten. Auch die weitschweifigen Wiederholungen und der abrupte Schluss sind ganz seine Weise. Die Denkschrift ist von besonderer Bedeutung durch das Datum zu Anfang und durch die gleichzeitig mit einer thätigen Gesetzgebung vorgetragenen Reformvorschläge. Sie begründet dieselben folgendermassen: König und Rath müssen darauf bedacht sein den seit 27 Jahren, d. h. seit Regierungsantritt Heinrichs VIII gesunkenen Wohlstand des Reichs wieder aufzurichten. Damit die Regierung reich werde, muss auch das Volk reich sein. Es ist daher zu erforschen, wie viel Gold und Silber sich im Lande befindet und wie viel jährlich von aussen eingeführt wird. Da aber der Wohlstand vor Allem aus der Arbeit entspringt, muss untersucht werden, wer und was der Arbeit schädlich entgegen wirkt. Wer nicht arbeitet, verdient nicht zu essen, wie die Schrift sagt; er sündigt und ist der Gnade ledig. Die beiden Productionsfactoren von Natur und Arbeit sind Ackerbau und Handwerk, ersterer, bei Weitem am bedeutendsten, um Lebensmittel, das Handwerk um Bezahlung hervorzubringen. Es wird daher eine genaue Aufnahme der Ackerbauzustände gefordert, damit wieder so viele Pflüge wie ehedem im Gang seien. Aber ebenso gilt es Handwerk und Gewerbe zu fördern, weil dadurch wieder allein das Geld dem Landbau zufliesst. In Wirklichkeit herrschen Armuth und Verbrechen, da jedes armen Mannes Sohn Kaufmann werden will, als solcher aber nur an sich, nicht an Nachbaren und Gemeinwohl denkt. Tuchmacher und andere Handwerker müssen in Städten leben. Nun führt aber der Handelstand deren Producte aus ohne Gold und Silber dafür zurückzubringen. Es sollen daher die Innungen der Tuchmacher und der Stapler aus ihren Urkunden nachweisen, was vor 124 Jahren die Wollpreise gewesen um sie auf den alten Fuss herabzusetzen und dadurch die Einhegungen wieder dem Ackerbau zu öffnen. Der Vorschlag geht ferner dahin das in den Landstädten angefertigte Tuch mit den respectiven Stadtsiegeln und, nachdem es in den Londoner Centralstapel eingeliefert, mit dem königlichen Stapelsiegel zu versehen um jedem Betrug im Auslande vorzubeugen. Nachweislich wird in Antwerpen und anderen Orten der Niederlande englisches Tuch fünf, sechs Ellen länger gestreckt und so mit dortigem aus englischer und spanischer Wolle gemischten Bastardtuch zum grossen Nachtheil der echten Waare nach Deutschland verkauft. Man muss den directen Einkauf gegen baares Geld wieder nach London verlegen. Da liesse sich um die viele fremde Münze vollwerthig auszugleichen mit dem königlichen Stapel ein Wechselgeschäft verbinden. Dann müssen aber auch die Merchant Adventurers denselben Ausfuhrzoll auf Tuch wie die Fremden und nicht 4 Schilling weniger entrichten. So wird das Geld wieder ins Land gezogen und durch Handwerk und Ackerbau dem eigenen Volke zugeführt. Dann brauchen auch König und Parlament nicht drückende Abgaben vom gemeinen Mann zu erheben, während jetzt allerlei fremde Waare, aber kein Geld ins Land kommt, das Volk darbt und die Regierung nicht einschreitet. Die traurige Lage des Volks sollte durch Parlamentsacte gebessert werden. Aber im Hause der Gemeinen sitzen gerade diejenigen, die jährlich 200000 Pfund dem Gemeinwohl entziehen und selber einstecken, Inhaber vieler Pachtländereien, die als Schafzüchter,

Handelsleute, Aufkäufer von Korn Alles nach Kräften vertheuern, und Advocaten, die nur Händel anschüren. Rettung ist allein bei König und Lords, wenn sie sich der Stadträthe versichern, damit das Geld wieder in Stadt und Land einströme und durch beider Arbeit vermehrt werde. Bereits aber wird der Lord, der einst glänzend Haus hielt, durch den Kaufmann zurückgedrängt. Man soll den Stapel zwingen zu den früheren niederen Preisen zurückzukehren und durch strenge Bestrafung des Betrugs Handwerk und Ackerbau erleichtern. Zum Sitz des Stapels und Wechsels in London wird Leadenhall empfohlen. Da in unterwerthiger Münze viel Geld ins Ausland geschleppt worden, soll man die schlechte fremde Courantmünze nicht verbieten, sondern mit fixiertem Werth umlaufen lassen. Vor Allem muss der König die Freiheit Londons an sich nehmen, weil sie von den Incorporierten zum Nachtheil der Gesammtheit ausgebeutet wird. Fremde müssen direct beim Stapel in London einkaufen dürfen. Zur Verpflegung Londons soll eine Summe ausgeworfen werden, damit den Aufkäufern von Korn, Vieh, Malz das Handwerk gelegt werde. London hat Geld genug dazu. Aber auch den anderen Städten ist es nützlich Summen zur Verfügung zu haben um Nahrungsmittel bei den Erzeugern selber einzukaufen. Der Verfasser möchte am liebsten allen Parlamentsacten ausweichen, weil sie im Unterhause von den verhassten Kaufleuten ausgehen, oft Söhnen armer Leute, die als Lehrlinge abgerichtet wurden auf den Profit von anderer Leute Arbeit zu speculieren. Der Kaufhandel zerstört den ganzen Wohlstand, weil er ohne Gewissen selber nur reich werden will und höchstens aus Furcht vor den Gesetzen die Advocaten befragt. Vom Wolltuch soll am Erzeugungsort ein G r o a t Abgabe entrichtet werden. Es lässt sich berechnen, dass durch solche Mittel für 400000 Mark des Jahrs mehr im Lande fabriciert wird. Auch Leinwand könnte zu Hause angefertigt, statt draussen gekauft werden. Auch wäre es rathsam das Geld nicht für Wein, Seide und anderes Gut der Fremde fort zu geben, sondern vorzugsweise für die von Alters her aus dem Osten bezogenen nützlichen Stoffe. Die englischen Kaufleute stehen dem Reichthum des Lands im Wege. Sehr willkommen waren die Osterlinge, ehe die Kölner in ihre Hanse aufgenommen wurden.

I.

A treatise concerninge the Staple and the Commodities of this Realme.

After the staplers hadd made theym self into a company corporat at Calais[1]) of no moo in nomber, than convenyently occupied so moche wolle and felles, as the housbond-men and fermours in England receyved of the gift of Godd yerly by werk of housbondry in a right order, wher Godd first gaff the leyrs[2]) therof, when no singularte was sought to have more plenty of wolle by mens wisdome, than God by his wisdome first ordenyd, that alle men by ther bodily werke schuld receyve of Goddes gift bothe mete and clothyng togeders, that is with the werke of housbondry to receyve the speciall gift of the fynes and goodness of the staple wolle, which Godd by his first day of everlastyng light by vertu of his holy spirit gaff into the erth for the comon welth of Englande, before sone moone and sters were made, whiche are but the mynesters of the gift of the same. Than at the first begynyng of the staple at Calais, whan was but a certayn number of staplers, than was the certayn quantite of staple wolle receyved of Godd by werk of housbondry ordynaryly sold at Caleis alwey for redy money and for bullion, which that tyme the Loo contreys in Flaunders was gladd to bryng to Calais to pay for wolle at the staple in hand, which bullion in a mynt at Caleis was coyned ther from the dayes of Richard the II^d duryng[3]) Henry the IIIIth[4]) the Vth[5]) and the VIth[6]) to Edward[7]) more than sixty[8]) yers, which was encrese of plenty of money to the holl welth of the reame, beside the clothe likwise for redy money was sold to straungers in the reame. After that soo many staplers encreased in number oon of a nother by meane of

---

1) Allmälich seit Ende des 14. Jahrhunderts, Macpherson, Annals of Commerce I, 604. 611.
2) Layer, Lage, Schicht.
3) 1377—1399.   4) 1399—1413.   5) 1413—1422.   6) 1422—1461.
7) IV, 1461.—1485.   8) Ms: XL^{ti}, offenbar verschrieben für LX^{ti}.

apprentishode withowt any consideracion of the welth of the holl reame, that in kyng Edwardes dayes the wolle that Godde yerly gaff to England by werke of housbondry, receyvyng clothyng with bodily levyng, was not able to suffise the nomber of staplers, which than was encresed, that sought in the reame to have staple wolle oon before a nother¹). Than begane the staplers to enhaunce the price of wolle, and oon to bye wolle before a nother begane to giff rewarde to fermours and to ther wiffes to have wolle oon before a nother. By reson so many staplers daily encreasyng somoch, the more wolle sought they daily to bye, as no merchaunt can bye withowt merchaundisez, wher than by meane of so many staplers occupieng so moche the more quantite of wolle, reysing the price of wolle, caused wolle to be the scarser and derer to the clothmakers. So the more staplers, that caridd the more staple wolle owt of the reame to Caleis, daily encreasyng the more quantite of wolle ther to selle, causid the lesse quantite of wolle remaynyng than in England to the use of the clothmakers. Yitt that tyme that begynnyng of distruccion of the reame was not espied, for than the first marte in the Loo countreis a this side Almaigne was holden in Brugge in Flaunders, when all nacions first resorted most comonly theder. That tyme Londoners hadde full recourse theder and gate riches plentuously, before so great nomber of adventurers than was not encreased as after was and now is. As all inordinate companyes made by mens wisdome, encreasyng into syngler weale, distroyeng comon weale, hath but a beeng and endyng for a certayn age, induryng swiche owt of a right contrary Goddes ordinancie cannot endure, like as no thyng under the sonne is of it self ever after but as vanyte.

At that tyme of kyng Edwarde²) Londoners beganne to pay costumes to the kyng by bryngyng straunge merchaundisez into the reame from

---

1) Schon 1476 galten sie als schlechte Zahler: marchauntes of the Estaple whyche at a prove ye shall fynde per case so slakke payers, that ye myght be deseyvyd ther by. I knowe dyverse have lost mony er they cowde gete ther dywtes owte off the Staple. Pasotn Letters, ed. J. Gairdner III, 166.

2) IV. 1461--1485.

the marte. That tyme Londoners scantly beganne first to adventure by south into Spayn. Crosby, that bilded his howse at Seynt Elens[1]), was ane of the first, that adventurid into Spayn so as upon a fourty four yere ago. Spayn was callid a farre adventure, and abowt a thirty six yere agoo was first occupieng to Turkye Scio and to all thos partes, alle which now are cowntid but as comon recourses, every nacion owt goyng a nothyr, every to oversayle by yonde other to seke syngularite. In example whether alle merchaundisez syns that tyme is not bought more derly and therof made more scarsite, moch wurse now in England than afore tyme was for the wealthe of the comonaltie, to see how it was never well syns regions and reames hath so farr sought oon to distroye the recourse and ordinarily levyng of another, to refourme the comon welth of all cristen reames lakkyth a right ordinary Emperour, which shuld take no righte of reames to be his right, but by the right wisdome of Godde shuld mynester the right that Godd to alle reames hath gevyn. Exemplum before Portyngale overseylid beyonde the equinoctiall to seke the rote, wher spices growith, to bryng the encrease therof into his singularite, of all tyme past the encrease therof of Goddes gift was earned upon lande from hande to hande, from oon contrey to a nother and solde by ordinary recourse by wey of staples, wherby the merchaunts every hadde ordinary wynnyng oon by another. Yhe, that tyme carryedd so long a wey in custodie from the staple at Venys thorowt Almaigne by marte into Flaunders, whan all reames bought it good chepe farre under the price that now is, for oon quarter of the value, that now is, of many thynges not nede to reherse herin: notmegges for 6 or 7^d the pownde not 30^{ti} yere agoo and gynger for 7^d, greyns for 6^d, clowz for 16^d, mace for 18^d, synamond for 18^d, suger $2\frac{1}{2}^d$, long pepper 8^d, saunders[2]) 10

---

[1] Sir John Crosby Wollhändler erwarb 1466 auf 99 Jahre ein Grundstück im Kirchspiel St. Helens, Bishopsgate, auf welchem er sein Haus mit einer heute noch erhaltenen stattlichen Halle erbaute. Er war 1470 Sheriff und Alderman der Stadt London, wurde 1471 von Eduard IV zum Ritter geschlagen und starb 1475. Stow, Survey of London p. 65.

[2] Sandelholz.

or 11^d, wher now it is to see, how the Portyngalez hath reised alle spices 3 parte more derer to the hurtyng the comon weale of all remes, after the kynde of merchaunts, as oon merchaunt to make hym self riche care not to hurt all other, as Portyngale for his singler weale hath distroyed the comon weale of gret nomber of peple by distroying the old recourse of spices, wherby every contry oon helpid another. And therby in conclusion now to see, how all reames cristen is hurt therby, which now cannot be reformyd but by a right Emperour, that cannot mynester right to every reame in as moche as he takith the righte of so many reamys by fleshly lynke to be his right.

Now lett us goo to the staplers at Caleis ageyn, whan it was well in England havyng no moo but so many as caried owt no more wolle and felles to the staple, than they receyvid for it redy money or bullion in hande, which than was coyned ther and daily brought into England. Than was vitalles and money in England and comon peple lyvyng the better by werke of husbondry, than alle the staplers of wolle and felles dwellid owt of London in the contreys abowt the reame, which occupied no straunge merchaundise, that with the money, that rose of ther wolle salez at Caleis, never returnid it into Englande in merchaundisez, but that tyme was coyned at Caleis so long tyme as abowt the later dayes of kyng Edward. So many staplers was encresid, for whose occupieng so moch the more staple wolle in England was encresid and brought to Caleis, that the Dowch tong perceyvid, they shuld never lakk non, but have it soo plentuous, which causid theym to forsake to pay redy money and bullion at the staple to bye it for respite. By that meanes the mynt in Caleis desolvyd, and so was it ordenyd, that the Dowch tong with the staplers concludid to pay for wolle but a certayn money in hande at the staple, and the residew to be payde at dayes apoyntid at the marte in the Loo contreys after the mart at Brugge desolvyd, and other marte was made at Andwarpe and Barow[1]) and Myddelborow[2]). Now take hedd after that conlusion a standard rate was made at Calis, how moche Fle-

---

1) Bergen op Zoom, Nord-Brabant.   2) Middelburg, Seeland.

mysh money shuld make the sterlyng pownde, abowt 28 shilling Flemysh the pownde, after which rate the staplers recyvyd ther payments for ther wolle at the marte. Which staplers after that tyme never usid for ther wolle to bryng no money into England, as they didd before, but alwey patisid¹) and covenauntid with the adventurers²) in London to delyver ther money, that rose of ther wolle sales to theym by exchaunge. So begane the staplers and the adventurers for ther own singler profite to make ther exchaunge to geders in kepyng owt of the reame all such mo-. ney, as yerly shuld be brought into the reame for our riche comodites, so as the kynge of England and alle the lordes of therth, the rulers of the peple, never syns hath serchid nor seen, how the comon weale of the reame hath been distroyed, nor never thynking of such maters, but loke forward and nothyng behynd in tyme past. But always whan hurte of peple is spied, that such as are hurt, of necessite compleyn, than rigour makyth acte, who, that dothe such hurte, and myschiefe, ageyn to have myschief for his reward, either payne, losse of godes or deth. That is rigorous lawe of after witt ever after mischief and hurte emonges the peple is wrought, the lordes in England hath ynow to doo to herken alwey to mischiefs doon in the reame dayly for lakk of a right order of lief in the holl comonaltie. But they never serche to the originall cause to know, what is the very rote of the holl nede, necessite and scarsite of the holl reame. Whan the Dowch tong hadd so aggred with the staplers of England to sett ther money at a certayn rate of 28 shilling the sterlyng pownde to pay so to the staplers at the marte, than ratid they ther money in ther contreys at the marte at hygher value, that rather than the staplers shuld carye ther money for ther wolle into England, they shuld gayn more profite to delyver it by exchaunge to adven-

1) D. i. kamen überein, cf. Halliwell, Dictionary of archaic and provincial words: patising.

2) Die Merchant Adventurers, obwohl auf älterer Vereinigung beruhend, wurden doch erst durch Acte Heinrichs VII. vom Jahre 1505 zu einer Compagnie incorporiert mit besonderer Vergünstigung, Wollzeuge in die Niederlande auszuführen, Macpherson, Annals of Commerce II, 27.

turers of London for 8^d or 12^d lesse in the pownde to wyne soo moche by that exchaunge in every pownde to receyve ther money, after they come home or sende into England at ther day to receyve it in London. Which money the adventurers of London, receyvyng it at the marte of the staplers, bestowith it ther upon all straunge merchaundise and bryngith it over into England, wher before that tyme the staplers for ther wolle brought ther money into England so long, as they sold ther wolle for redy money at the staple and kept a mynt ther.

Now see another exchaunge, that the staplers than beganne to make with the adventurers in London. After such constitucion made of wolle to be sold for respite, and the money therfor paid at marte was sold at the staple by ther tyme of ages brought theder, the staplers in England apoyntid to receyve ther payments in such wise at marte, consideryng ther shyppyng of wolle in England, thought to wyne more by the age of ther wolle brought to Caleis, than to receyve ther money them self at the marte to make it over first into England and afterward therwith to bye ther woll and so lose a shippyng, hadd lever lose the profite of ther exchaunge beyonde see to receyve so moch money in London of the adventurer, therwith to bye wolle to save a shippyng and wyn so moche more money by the age of ther wolle at Caleis, and the adventurer therfor to receyve the money owyng to the stapler at the marte. Thus by theis two kyndes of exchaunges never was brought into England no money, for English wolle sold at the staple. after wolle was sold for respite in Flaunders, and by the exchaunge betwen the stapler and merchaunt adventurer in London is double losse to the kyng and his lordes and the holl reame. For so doth the adventurer delyver his stokk of money to the stapler, which elles he shuld bestow upon clothes, that is the kynges comodites, therfor to pay the kynges costome by carieng it owt of the reame, wherof the kyng losith his costome. And that adventurer so doyng make his exchaunge goth over see with an empty haude, and receyvith the staplers money beyonde see and ther bestowith it upon straunge merchaundise and bryngith it into the reame, which elles by the stapler ought to be brought into the reame in redy money. In this wise beganne the exchaunge betwen staplers and adventurers of London, after the wolle at Caleis was sold for respite. And by the said reason so moch wolle was sold that tyme to the townes in Holand and other contreys for respite, takyng ther town scales for sewertie, which by the werrs, that Fredrik the Emperour that tyme made in Flaunders for Maximylian his sone¹), by destroyeng such townes and the peple in theym the kynges staple lost great somes of money, that never after was hadd nor recovered to the gret hynderaunce of the holl reame. And from that tyme to this tyme by the same makyng of exchaunge the staplers and adventurers hathe kept owt of the reame all such money gold and silver, which elles for wolle and cloth shuld yerly come into the reame. Over long processe herin to discribe, how they have distroyed the comon weale of the holl reame by the ignoraunce and sufferaunce of the kyng and of his lordes.

Alwey to see and consider, how the rote of most myschief hath ever bredd in London, wher as all staplers was first owt of London, dwellyng abrode in the reame unto within sixty yeres agoo, that than the staplers toke into ther folish adventurers of London by redempcion. After they soo dydd, the adventurers by ther occupieng of byeng all straunge merchaundise of the martes hadd so moche the more advauntage over the staplers of the countrey, that in short processe of tyme begane to were owt all the staplers abrode in the reame. Now take hedde, after adventurers in London became to be staplers, all the staple wolle in the reame was not able to suffise theym. Than begane the rank myschyff and distruction of the holl reame to spryng and sprede owt of London duryng this fourty yers past and more. Than begane so many byers of wolle in all contreys callid broggers²) and not staplers nor clothmakers, but such as gate it owt of pore mens hands and ferms to sell it to the staplers in London for coynne of money. Than began the price of wolle to rise so hygh more and more daily, that fermours alwey metyng at marketts, as

---

1) Der niederländische Krieg von 1488 ist gemeint.
2) Brokers, Mäkler.

alle sorts mete like to like, oone heryng of another the highnes of the
price of wolle so risyng stodyed and devisid, how to destroy mens werks
of housbondry to encrese more wolle, therof to have the more plenty.
So rose the price of wolle so hyghly, that in conclusion fermours, yhe,
and gentilmen began to putt ther erthe to idulnes, makyng pasture to
fede more shepe to encrease the more staple wolle, in so moch as they
beganc to serche and stody ther wisdome to accownt the gret profite,
that they myght wynne therby, serchyng owt the leyrs of the grownd,
wherin Godd gaff his gifft of fyne wolle, either fermours, that of the lordes
cowd gete erth in ferme by leisz, or the lordes of the erthe theym selfes,
perceyvyng such singularites, made ther accownts. First accowntyng, how
moch money the yerly rent of a holle village or towne was worthe, wher
goode leyir of wolle was, which rent per adventure past not a 40 or 50
pownde by yere, wherupon a 400 peple hadde labours and lyvyng by
werks of housbondry, daily encresyng bredyng and bryngyng forth of
plenty of corn and catall with ther bodily labours, every with other lyvyng
owt of nede and necessite, and over that paid the yerly rent to the lord
truly and lyvid in forme of Crist, as members of his body shuld live in
a holy chirch in cure of mystery of his holy spirit, mynestrid by a persone
havyng cure over sole and body. Upon such serche of the yerly rent
of such villages and townes accowntid, how many acres within the pre-
cinct therof and how great nomber of shepe it was able to fede, being
made idull and put to pasture, and how moche wolle thos shepe wolde
yerly encrease and how moch money that wolle was worth after so hygh
price reisid, that in conclusion they fownd soo gret yerly profits by the en-
creaseng of wolle more than by occupieng the erth with the werks of
husbondry for the meyntenaunce of comon peple, that causid them for
ther own singler weale to breke down all the howsis and howsholdes[1]
puttyng the dwellers owt from ther labours and levyng to seke ther

---

[1] Wie die Gesetzgebung Heinrichs VII. und Heinrichs VIII. dagegen einzuschreiten suchte, führt aus E. Nasse, Die mittelalterliche Feldgemeinschaft und die
Einhegungen des sechszehnten Jahrhunderts in England, Bonn 1869. p. 56. 57.

lyvyng as in wildernes wanderyng by beggyng and stelyng or otherwise to gete ther mete, wher they can. And the curats of all such villages and townes not consederyng the worde of God, how all peple shulde werke to receyve ther levyngs of Godds gift in right order. as Adam was first putt into paradise, that he shuld werke. And Poule saith: who will not werke, that he ete not[1]). And he saith: every man shuld werke in pece to ete his own mete[2]), that no man shuld ete awey his neighbours mete, but werk to deserve his own mete, before he ete it[3]), and that no man for his mete shuld distroy the werks of Godd[4]). Alle theis texts of Goddes wordes the curats never oons serchid nor remembrid nor never ledd ther peple to such cure, but for their tyme wer contentid to take of the lorde of the soile as moch yerly, as he was able to reise clerly over all charges of his offis mynestrid in his cure to putt that in his persone and bere a hawk on his fist and a spaynyall teyd to his taile or a little biche to hunt the wall[5]), and lett alle his shepe ronne astray and seke ther lyvyng, wher they lustid, to ete up every mans corne, what so ever myschief shuld chaunce theym carid not. Now see, what myschief all such pasturers of shepe wrought to encrease more staple wolle than God ordenyd, what dewlish[6]) wisdome rotid in theym. they wrought ageynst Goddes ordinaunce in that his worde saithe: *anima plus quam corpus et corpus plus quam vestimentum*[7]). For the lesse profite they distroyd the more for singler lucre, by encresyng wolle for clothyng they distroyd bodily levyng, and by distroyng the lyvyng of the body causid the peple of necessite to sete theyr lyvyng to the distruccion of ther solles, and what other examples are to see, how they have wrought to distroy the ordinaunce of Godde and his werkes, for oon thyng hath distroyed another.

---

1) Thessal. II, 3. 10.   2) Ibid. v. 12.   3) Ibid. v. 8.
4) Rom. 14. 20 Noli propter escam destruere opus Dei.
5) Schon 1390 untersagte ein Parlamentsstatut den Priestern und Klerikern unter 10 Pfund Jahreseinkommen einen Hund zu halten, „leverer, n'autre chien". 13 Ric. II. c. 13, Stubbs, Constitutional History of England III, 538.
6) devilish.   7) Matth. 6, 25.

What wikkyd dewlish bestes are they, that may see, how Godd made all thynges by his wisdome, and if Godd hadd foresene and thought it more wisdome to have gevyn his speciall giftes of fynes and goodness of staple wolle to any moo places of the erth in England, than to thos, to which he at the first begynnyng ordenyd and made, he myght as well have made all the erth in England to yeld staple wolle as thos certayn places, whych he ordenyd. What wretchis are thos, that for ther own syngler weale werkith ageynst Goddes wille and ordinaunce to distroy the comon weale of the holl reame. All trew Cristen peple may feithfully beleve by ther wisdom to stryef ageynst Goddes wisdome by ther werkes to ete ther mete in distroyng Goddes werkes, than to werke to receyve any thyng in this world otherwise, than Godd hath ordenyd and yerly gyveth it owt of hevyn. Who jugith in hymself to doo that thyng, that is contrary to Godd, is sync withowt faith, not worthy to receyve at the fest of pasch the body of Crist.

Many folish erronyous opynyons and arguments hathe bene and is emonges wikkyd peple. Some saith: so moch wolle in England hathe bene more than nede, that for the comon weale is said, it hathe bene buruyd. Staplers now a daies to show ther myschief to be profitable to the reame saith: if they caried not so moche wolle owt of the reame, elles it shuld be lost not able to drape it. They say also: that Spanysh wolle is so encresid to fynes goodness and so great plenty, that withowt they holp to sell our English wolle, elles non other reame shuld have nede to bye it in England. And further they say and hold an opynyon, that by carieng certayn shepe owt of England into Spayn by kyng Edwardes dayes, that by the bodyes of the shepe then robbid England of our speciall gift of fynes and goodnes of our staple wolle. With such vayn void resons they fill mens wittes. But the trouth is to see, how Godd gaff that speciall gift of fynes of goode wolle in the erthe, before sonne moone and sters and before man was made, which gift comyth of Godd from above man. This is over mens wisdome and power of this worlde to robbe England of that gift God the gever and all his ordinary mynesters of the gift in hevyn is evyn like now as ever hath ben in like force and effect. In exemplum to see in England, wherin oon ayre heyt and temperaunce, is the shepe fedyng on the erthe, wher is a fyne leyre of staple woll; within a myle or two is a corse leyre of heyry wolle; to shere of the wolle of the shepe of bothe leyr and chaunge the shepe, puttyng either sort of the shepe on others leyre. Ther next flesh of ther wolle shall grow after the gift of the leyr. So as the removyng of the shepe removith no part of Goddes gift gevyn into the erthe. No, nor if the very erbe, wherby the shepe receyve ther fedyng, shuld be paryd up by the rotes and chaunged either to the others leyre, the erbe is no mater, wherby to remove Goddes speciall gift of fynes and goodnes of wolle in the erthe. So as all speciall gift of riche comodites, that Godd first gaff into the erth in every reame to oon reame, that another hath not, to the entent, that every reame shuld be able to liff of Goddes gift, oon to be help to another to be an occasion oon to live by another. All such gifts Godd by his spirit in the first day of everlastyng light gaff theym into the erthe, before makyng lights of this world sonne moone and sters, in as moche as it is to see, how they are but the mynesters of thos gifts. Like as Godd ordenyd all men to werke the meate, that the sone of man shall gyve us, whom Godd the father hath sealid, so is the sonne the greate brode seale of Goddes rightwisnes, wherby Godd by the sonne in his office contynually and dayly ledethe all erthly bodyes to werke, goyng from the este to the west, and in his other office from the south to all and to every reame region and countrey, his gift every yere, which Godd in the first begynnyng gaff into erthe. Which gyft is over and above mans compas by no mans power nor wisdome oon reame to robbe another of all suche giftes, as Godd by the office of sone of man gevyth to all men.

In exemplum elles every reame hadd robbid another or this day: England havyng the fynest woll, if it had wolle oyles, that Godd hath gevyn to Spayn and other contreys, than wole England sette nought be Spayn. It is to see, how every reame hath serchid to robbe oon another. England hath geten owt of Spayn and other contreys the roth and fruyts of olives figges almonds dates and orynges and such other thyngs and hath sette and plantid theym in the erth in England, which hath brought forth to bodyly stokk and braunchis and levys by the risyng of the sonne in the spryng of the yere. But whan the sonne comyth to the mystery of his gift at mydsomer, beholdyng England soo willyng to robbe Spayn to gete from it Goddes gifts, the sonne turnyth from the northe towards the southe and will not giff no vertu of good to non of the comodites of Spayn, soo removid into England, nother ripnes swetnes stength in operacion, nor no propertie, that shuld help and encrease England to the hurt and hynderaunce of Spayn. So evident to see, how the office of the sonne is not only to mynester alle the gifts of Godd yerly to every reame region or contrey on the erthe accordyng like as Godd in the first begynnyng gaff it, but also the sonne by his office holdith and kepith every reame and contrey in his own right, that noo oon robbe nor hurte another. What a lorde is Godd, that so rightwisly mynesterith right to all reames and contreis rownd abowt all the holl erthe by his oonly oon great brode seale of his law of sone of man, gevyng mete for bodily levyng to all men in this world, as in John VI°: *operamini cibum, quem filius hominis dabit vobis; hunc enim pater signavit*[1]) etc. What a wisdome is of erthly kynges, that in oon litle reame, which is but as a howse in comparison of the kyngdom of sone of man, that in so litle quantite cannot giff to every man right and kepe every man in his right by oon ordinary hedd-seale, but for a sory cotage of a noble rent by yere must have many writyngs and many sealis, and therby can nother see nor know, how to have right clerly nor suerly. Soo false is mens wisdome and policy.

It may well be said: in England is no right order, wher all and every man sekith the policy ageynst the ordynaunce of Godd oon to robbe another in distroyng the holl welth of the reame, to see, how the pastures of shepe to encrease so great quantite of wolle to suffice the inordinat nomber of staplers in the reame, which within a sixty yers hath distroyed a 400 or 500 villages in the myddell parts of the body of the reame[2]).

---

1) Evang. Joh. VI, 27.
2) Ganz ähnlich Cardinal Pole in Starkey's Dialogue p. 72: And ther, wher hath

A mervelous sight to see, England for lakke of the lyvely grace of Godd lyveth like as a beste, which, beeng woundyd of the sere greff and smert, the members hath sensible felyng, but of the cause therof they have no descrivyng. So the pore wrechid bestly membris of the body of the reame, every meting with other in company, compleynyth of ther sore greff of nede and necessite of vitalls clothyng and money. They sensibly fele scarsite, so lyvyng in mysery. But they know not the cause therof which causith theym to murmur and grudge daily, redy to doo any myschief, if they thought, it myght be any remedy. Such mysorder in the reame is not convynyent in the body of a kyng[1]) An exemplum is to see, how within a sixty yers, that Londoners hath become staplers, oon stapler in London hath distroyd the labours and levyng of 4000 or 5000 comen peple and hath distroyd the plenty of vitall of the holl reame, wher Godd hath ordenyd by his gift, that comen peple shuld werk to receyve no more staple wolle yerly, than of thos shepe, to the which Godd gevith lieff on such leyrs, wher staple wolle are, to be therupon bredd and brought up by werke of husbondry. So as all peple shuld werke the erthe to receyve both mete for bodily levyng and clothyng togeders, not for clothyng to distroy bodily levyng, for the lesse to distroy the more. That wisdome is of the dewlis[2]) depe witt owt of the depist risyng. But so they have distroyd village and the labours and lyvyng of comen peple. Some oon pasturer of shepe for his own singularite hath

byn many housys and churchys, to the honowre of God, now you shal fynd no thyng but schypcotys and stabullys, to tho ruyne of man; and thys ys not in one place or two, but generally throughout thys reame.

1) Schon in More's Utopia p. 28 ed. Glasgow 1750 sagt Raphael: oves vestrae, quae tunc mites esse, tamque exiguo solent ali, nunc (ut fertur) tam edaces atque indomitae esse coeperunt, ut homines devorent ipsos, agros, domos, oppida vastent et depopulentur. Später Latimer in der Predigt am 8. März 1549, Works I, 100: For where as have been a great many householders and inhabitants, ther is now but a shepherd and his dog: so they hinder the king's honour most of all. Ueber die Acte 25 Henr. VIII. c. 12. 13 (1533. 1534) und ihre Fruchtlosigkeit Nasse l. c. 57. 58.

2) the devil's.

distroyedd howsis and howsholdes and labours and levyngs of a 1000 or 1200 or 1400 peple, and, after the erth in villages so putt to idulnes and pasture, hath hadd no shepe of that bredyng therupon to have fedyng, but to ete the gresse.

To encrease wolle hath alwey usid to bye the shepe [from][1]) alle heyry corse leyrs in Walys and other owtbredyng and bryng theym to the good leyrs, wher ther corse wolle chaungith to staplewolle, but not so pure fyne wolle, like as in old tyme it was receyvid by werks of housbondry. Forasmoch as the speciall gift therof is in the erthe, therfor the shepe to receyve that gift of fynes and godnes therof must nedes fede of the leyres of the erthe, like as in old tyme the erth was wrought and openyd by tillage, that the shepe myght fede of the inward leyre of the erth and therupon nyghtly lay and was foldydd. Than receyvid the shep ther naturall fedyng of the leyre of fyne staple wolle, evyn like Godd first gaff it. So as than was it pure fyne woll oon pownd worth two now, because the erthe is now put to idulnes to bryng forth rank foggye wild gresse, wherupon the shepe of the hyghest of the gresse receyvith ther fedyng. so receyve they rank wild heyry wolle, in that they cannot come to the leyr of therthe, owt therof to receyve the gift of Godd.

So is the gift of fyne wolle yerly lost to the great hurt and sclander of the reame, that is the cause, that now of late years peple comonly reportith: Spaynysh woll is almost as good as English woll, which may well be soo, by that Spayn hath housbondid ther wolle frome wurse to better, and England from better to wurse, which must nedes cause theym the nygher to accorde to oon godnes. Yitt can they not be lyke by Goddes ordinaunce. English wolle hath staple and Spaynysh wolle hath no staple. So as Spayn hath assayed all the meanes to cause ther wolle to have staple, washyng ther woll upon the shepe before sheryng, and washyng it after sheryng, can have no staple by Goddes own ordinaunce, albeit Spayn hath bettrid ther wolle by shiftyng of leirs and by hous-

---

1) fehlt in der Handschrift.

bondry and within a fifty yers hath encreasid so moche wolle, which by a staple holden in Brugge in Flaunders sellyng six tymes more now, than of old tyme, that is drapid with English wolle in Flaunders and all the Loo contreis so plentifully settyng ther comon peple to werke and English peple to liff idully. English wolle myxid with Spaynysh wolle makyth soo great quantite of clothe, that distroyth the sale of all English cloth, so as all, that English merchaunts doth with the comodites of the reame, is to the distruction of all comon peple. And an example is to see the wolles of Spayn are of such kynds withowt the wolles of England be myxed with, it can make no clothe of it self for no durable weryng to be nother reisid nor dressid, by cause it hath no staple. Spaynish wolls are of diversite of leyrs of fynes and corsnes of the heyres. Some will make clothe of fyne drapyng worthe a 12 shilling or a marc[1]) a yarde with laboure, albeit it shall have no staple in the weiryng like English clothe. In short tyme the wolle shall were awey unto the likness of worstedd[2]) notwithstanding the fynes and goodnes of English wolls thus distroyed by reason of distroyng housbondry with the labours and levyng of comon peple.

Only for the singler lucre of the pasturers of the shepe they have distroyed the comen weale to encrease so moche quantite of staple wolls to susteyn the staplers latly risen in London, which now hathe distroyd alle other staplers in the holl reame. To see the customable usage of pasturers of shepe, that alwey to store ther pastures hathe usid to remove all the store of the owtbredyng of shepe in Wales and other places to ther staple leyrs, to encrease staple wolle. Which shepe, so removid from their fedyng on the hygh mowntayns and hilles in Wales to the rank fedyng on the leyrs of staple wolle, hath so rottid and distroyd the store of the shepe of the holl reame of so long tyme usid, that the pasturers by experience can make ther rekonyng of alle sorts of shepe of diversites of ther bredyng, how long every sort shall liff on ther growuds, forcyng no thyng of the rottyng of ther bodyes, because the price of the

---

1) Alte Münzrechnung = 13 sh. 4 d.　　　　　2) Kammwollgarn.

wolle are now as moche more as in the old tyme. Therfor, if the pasturers may have a two or three flesis of the woll and the felles, they force not of the bodyes, but whan the rott comyth, in as short a tyme as they can sell theym to brochers for little more, than the felles are wurthe, rather so to ridd theym in such wise, as the great nomber of rottyn shepe hathe ben eten in England, which in old tyme was wont to ete on ther own bredyng and lyvid in helth ther full age, brought thorowt the reame by faires and markets to sell for 16 ͡ a weder, that now is worthe 4 shilling, and than twenty shepe for oon now, and than more sweter muttons which on heyry leyrs are swetter, than on fyne leyrs. Thus the idulnes of the erth and the ranke gresse hathe bothe distroyd the fynes of the wolls and rottid the shepe, that some oon pasturer losith a 12000 or 16000 shepe in oon yere and alwey storith his pastures agayn with owtward breding. So as some yere a 1000 shepe is rottid in England, that was wont to be eten for the vittallyng of all comon peple in the reame, that no marvell is of scarsite of vitall. And in so moche as beff and mutton is made scarse, all other vitalle must nedes be scarse[1]).

What a myschief dothe every oon of such pasturers werke in the reame in oon village to distroy the labours and levyng of a 400 or 500 of comen peple, and all the bredyng and encresyng of corn and catalls therin and in distroyng so many shepe, as from ther own grownds are brought to all such grownds, wher no man is fedd of the gresse, that Godd yerly gyvith theim, and all the gresse, wher all suche shepe shuld ete on ther own grownds, wher they wer bredd, yerly rottith on the grownds ther, wher no catall is, like as was in old tyme to ete it. So is almost the half of the sustynaunce of the holl reame distroyd, which Godd givith is not receyvid of his gift, but byers and sellers by such

---

1) Wherfor, when they are closyd in ranke pasturys and butful ground, they are sone touchyd wyth the skabe and the rotte; and so, though we nurysch over many by inclosure, yet over few of them (as experyence schowyth) come to the profyte and use of man. Lupset in Starkey's Dialogue p. 98.

polycy werkyth to receyve ther levyng by the robbyng and destroyng of the holl comonaltie. And all this myschieff of the pasturers is wrought to encrese staple wolle to susteyn the inordinate nomber of staplers, as ther can be no theffes withowt receyvours, so as in reformyng staplers shall reforme pasturers.

An exemplum is to see, how some oon stapler is the causer of the distruction of a 4000 or 5000 comon peples levyng. Oon stapler in London will occupie as moche wolle, as is encreasid owt of the distruction of 4 or 5 villages, wher a 1400 or 1500 peple hathe hadde labours and levynge, and that wolle caried owt of the reame to the hyndryng of as many, which elles shuld drape it and to help so many in other contreys. And all the money, that ryseth of the sales of the same wolle beyend see, is ther bestowid upon artificiall thynges brought into England, which distroyeth as many mens labours and levyng, which elles shuld make it here the kyng and his lords, no thyng consideryng that myschief, which pore artificiall peple hathe ben therewith sorely grevid and therupon hath compleynyd withowt remedy. Always whan handcrafty men hath compleynyd upon Londoners, that are adventurers, which hath brought all wares into England of the occupacions sleytly made for litle price, wher with they have fillid full the holl reame to pore hanydcrafts mens distructions. Merchaunts alwey causith the kyng and his lords beleve, they do it for the welth of the reame, reportyng, English men cannot make it so goode chepe and will not werke, but giff ther bodyes to slouthe, etyng and drynkyng, and so blaspheme ther own naturall neighbours, and theym self beeng the causers, that all artificiall peple in London and elles wher in England now cannot make artificialite so good chepe as in old tyme, in as moch as they like as afore sayd hath distroyd ther plenty of bodyly lyvyng and also they have usid to bryng so great abundaunce of all artificiall thyngs into England so sleytly made for so litle money, distroyng all artificers, that no man can use exarcise or actyvite of artificialite approvid. If any English man wold stody to devise and invent any new artificiall thynges, Londoners incontynent is ever redy to destroy it. Abowt a fourteen yers past was but a sleyt fantasy devised in Kent of makyng the first bedys with the pater noster[1]) holow like muske balles, made of boxe, which in a short tyme susteynyd a 30 or 40 men, that made theym and sold theym to Londoners, wherby all parties, which occupied theym, gate lyvyng oon with another unto a haburdasher, that caried a sample into Flaunders and ther causid a gret abundaunce of theym to be made by yong prenters[2]) used in all such actyvite ther and brought theym into England to the distruction of the seid artificers here.

Thus adventurers hath usid by bryngyng of straunge artificialite owt of Flaunders to distroy all artificialite in England, wherby the kyng and his lords are made scarse of money, not consideryng ther welth nor the welth of the holl reame. The holl welthe of the reame is for all our riche comodites to gete owt of all other reamys therfore redy money; and after the money is brought in to the holl reame, so shall all peple in the reame be made riche therwith. And after it is in the reame, better it were to pay 6^d for any thyng made in the reame than to pay but 4^d for a thyng made owt of the reame, for that 6^d is owres so spent in the reame and the 4^d spent owt of the reame is lost and not ours, if a right order of a comon weale may be said in England to have vitall as plentifull as in old tyme artificialite to be meyntenyd shall cause as good chepe artificialite as in other reames and moche more substaunciall. It shall be the gret welth to the kyng and all his lords to sett as moche peple as can be to artificialite, for as moch as they labour and werke all for money, that ther money may alwey ronne owt of ther hands in to the hands of such, as occupieth housbondry for ther mete and drynk, which money shuld so ronne owt of the housbonds hands into the hands of the kyng and of his lords of the erth. As it is convenyent for lords to have plenty both of vitalle and of money, which Londoners hath distroyd and yut the lords discrivyth[3]) not ther own hynderaunce and losse.

1) beads, Rosenkränze.
2) prenter, printer, Drucker? vielleicht prentis für apprentice, Lehrbursche, Geselle.
3) für discerneth.

The bredyng of so many merchaunts in London, rison owt of pore mens sonnes, hath ben a mervelous distruction to the holl reame, wher first worshipfull men bownd ther yong children to be merchaunts in London, unto[1]) so many were bownd prentisses, that ther masters wold never giff theym no wages, after they cam owt of ther termes, and than havyng no frends to giff theym nor lend theym a stokke of redy money to occupie their occupacion, that is ther instrument to occupie byeng and sellyng of merchaundise, nor havyng no handy crafte, wherby to gete ther levyng with no instruments on hande, must nedes lose all ther tyme of prentishod and their yougth, than to seke theym some other lyvyng to be a servytour by some other meane, or elles to seke to bye merchaundises for respite to gete a stokke to begyn with by such meanes. So wer all yong merchaunts comyng owt of ther prentishod and cowd have no wages of ther masters compellid to borow clothes of clothe makers for respite, and caried the same clothes to the marts beyende see to sell, and ther must nedes sell theym and the money to bestow it on wares to bryng some to sell to make money to pay ther creditors at ther dayes. So abowt a fifty yers agoo such yong merchaunts begane to encrease in nomber[2]), that bought so many clothes of clothmakers for respit and sold theym in Flaunders at the martes of goode chepe to make retorn to pay ther creditours, that in short tyme they distroyed the price of wollen clothes, causyng all the old merchaunts to fall from byeng and sellyng clothes. The old merchaunts by encreasyng so many yong merchaunts by ther defawt never wold ordeyn non other remedy to help the yong men from such nede to distroy the sale of clothe to take fewer prentises and to giff theym wages or by some other meane to make order, that non shuld be bownden prentis to be merchaunts by such worshipful mens sonnes, as wer able to giff theym substaunce to bye and sell withowt nede of suche borowyng for dayes. But all ther masters the olde

1) für until.
2) Ganz ähnlich Cardinal Pole in Starkey's Dialogue p. 84: Merchantys, caryng out thyngys necessary for our owne pepul are overmany; and yet they wych schold bryng necessarys are to few.

merchaunts dispitfully wold defame such yong merchaunts, sayng, they wold be merchaunts, but for a little while so to hurt ther credence rather to undo them than help theym. And all straunge merchaunts in Flaunders, perceyvyng the necessite of the seid yong merchaunts, sought the weys daily, how to bye ther clothis good chepe. Than began old merchaunts to forsake occupieng of clothes to occupie ther money by exchaunge, which is not only pleyn usary, but also it hath and yitt doth helpe to distroye the welth of the kyng of his lords and comons, for that occupieng hynderith the reame bothe weys owtward and inward.

In exemplum the exchaunger owtward sekith either the stapler or straunger, that hath any money beyend see payable, and lakkith money here in England to be fayne to take money to his losse, for an English noble to giff a 4 or 5^d the more for a five or six wekes respit to be paid ageyn at the mart of Flaunders. So dothe such exchaungers never bestowe ther money upon no English clothe nor other thyngs, wherby to wyne money as upon merchaundise owtward to pay any custome to the kyngs profite or for any profite of the reame, but only to wyne lucre as upon the loone and forberyng of his money. After which money so receyvid agayn in Flaunders with the gayn therof, sekith owt adventurers of London, who will receyve that money agayn to bestowe it upon straunge merchaundisez to bryng it in to England and for the loone of every noble to giff as moche wynyng to the exchaunger ageyn. In such wise rich old merchaunts, many men seeng the price of clothe and the daunger and trouble of byeng strange merchaundises is so casuall for a more ease and lesse labour, they thus occupie ther money by exchaunge, wynnyng profite bothe inward and owtward, which is pleyne usary. Albeit they say, it is non usary, by reason, they say, they putt ther money in adventure, which adventure is not upon the see nor otherwise, but like as usary is accowntid usary to wyne profite by lendyng of money, seeng every such exchaunge for any some of money so lent by the name of exchaunge hath two billes obligatory for payment therof. Oon bill is to cary it over the see, wherby to receyve such money ageyn beyend see at the marts, and that other bill the exchanger kepith it for his sewertie in England to be sewer, if that other first bill shuld chaunce to be lost by adventure over the see, so as no colour of excuse can be made of puttyng such money in adventure, but as money lent by very kynd of usary havyng fewer bonds obligatory therefore.

Now to shew more of the said yong merchaunts, so many usid to borow clothes of clothe makers for respite duryng a fourteen or fifteen yers, in which tyme many of theym ranne awey to sayntwaries[1]) and other places, by lossis and lendyng not able to pay for theyr clothes, wher than clothe makers wold no longer trust to theym, but sought to sell ther clothes rather for money and wares to be poned[2]) in hand. Than begane clothe makers abowt a thirty six yers agoo to proferre ther clothes to Esterlyngs in the Stiliard[3]), whiche afore that tyme bought all ther clothes of merchaunts within the citie, by whome many citizens hadd gret gaynes and never sought to bye ther clothes of clothe makers. For a sixty yers agoo old merchaunts bought all ther clothes of cloth makers in the contrey by the holl sortes in pakkes brought home to ther howsis in carts and in wayns, whan than all sailyng clothes came never to Blakwell Hall[4]) to no Esterlyngs handes. But after clothmakers cowd not sell ther clothes nother to old merchaunts nor to yong merchaunts for ther suertie nor profite that causid theym this thirty yere and more to professe theym to sell to the Esterlyngs, so as the Esterlyngs syns that tyme hathe hadde clothes at ther pleasure for respite, that many of theym hath ronne awey with gret stokkes so borowid of clothe makers soome oon with a 3000 or 4000 pownde, and all for lakke of a right order, that English clothes are not sold to all straungers by wey of a staple for the comon weale of the holl reame.

1) Sanctuarien, Asyle.   2) pawned.
3) Der Stahlhof, die alte Gildhalle der Deutschen in London am linken Themseufer oberhalb London Bridge, s. J. M. Lappenberg, Urkundliche Geschichte des hansischen Stahlhofs in London, Hamburg 1851.
4) Blackwell, auch Bakewell Hall, in Basinghall Street, wo seit 20 Richard II (139^6/$_7$) ein Wochenmarkt für Wollzeuge stattfand, Cunningham, Handbook of London p. 28.

Yhe, and what a more myschieff hath such lendyng of clothe to the Esterlyngs causid yerly, wher in old tyme they brought great abundaunce of gold and silver in to the reame, now this many yers bryng they non.

To understand ther are two Haunces of the Esterlyngs: oon is the olde Haunce of the Sprusyners¹), that owt of the cold contreys in the este parties wher is frost and snow on eight monthis in the yere. They come but oons in the yere, bryngyng ther nedfull comodites for England: pitche tarre bowstavis wex flesh and such other. And what they hadd nede of more wollen clothe than England hadd nede of ther comodites, therfor they wer wont to bryng gold and silver uncoyned, wherof the name of sterlyng silver rose. But to understand that other Haunce is of the Esterlyng merchaunts of the Hausteddes in Almayn²). They do England moche hurt, as they be so sufferd, wer wont to bryng most gold and Suasburgh³) logges of silver into England. They carye owt of England clothes great quantite all the tymes in the yere. And comonly they will non bye but white only spone weyvid and fullid withowt any other werkmanship, wherwith they sett ther own peple to werk. And wher they have no comodites of Almayn to bryng into England for all such clothes, for which they were wont to bryng great plenty of gold and silver, they have usid more than thirty yers for ther clothes to bryng over all maner straunge aliaunt⁴) merchaundisez of all contreys: wode of Spayne, alyme of Ytaly, mader of Flaunders, yhe, and silke lynyn clothe and all other merchaundisez from the marts in Flaunders to delyver to clothe makers for clothes and to sell to Londoners to pay clothemakers, so as they never bryng no more gold and silver into the reame. So is England in such maner alwey stuffid storid and pesterid so full of straunge merchaundise, that as well English merchaunts and Esterlyngs hathe so usid the clothmakers to giff mony and wares for clothes, that clothmakers so takyng wares hathe pesterid all pore comon peple with

---

1) Prussians. Preussen.
2) Schon der Libell of English Policye unterschied zwischen zwei Hansen, Einleitung p. 10 u. v. 279. 280.
3) Schwaz in Tirol.   4) alien.

wares and litle money, that litle money is to be fownd in the holl reame, which must nedes cause litle store of money to the use of the kyng and of his lords.

Evyn like as cloth makers are usid, evyn like wise use they ther pore artificer, sayng to ther spynners carders weyvers fullers shermen and other: if they will have any werks, therfore they must take both wares and money as lynnen cloth and canvas for kerchews smokks and such other necessaryes and dubletts and jakkett clothes and all such other straunge wares for ther apparell, very scant for all pore peple to gete money to pay ther lords rents. It is over long to describe the myschief, that merchaunts werkth thorowt the reame by bryngyng such quantite of strange merchaundise and artificiall fantasies brought into the reame, that causith so great nomber of idull peple to fall to byeng and sellyng therof, so many pedlers and chapmen, that from fair to fair, from markett to markett carieth it to sell in horspakks and fote pakks in basketts and budgetts sitting on holydays and sondais in chirche porchis and in abbeys dayly to sell all such trifells[1]), wherby all straungers in other reames hath werk, and English men hath non, which in a right order myght make all kynde of artificialite nedfull to suffise the holl reame. All nacions sittyng in the contreys deviseth fantasies to make English men foles to gete the riches owt of the reme in experience as well French men and other, that in London shewith ware howsis full of trifell sold and bought for a hundred pownde, if the werkmanship of makyng therof takyn awey, the very substance beside the werk is not worth a hundred shilling. But boones hornes sakkes ledder peces heres papers erthyn potts botells glassis and such other trifells, yhe, and daily carieth owt of England old shoes hornes and bones, and bryngith it into the reame ageyn made in to fantasies, werby they gete the riches owt of the reme and not therfore take clothe nor English comodites, but sekith to have rialles, angels[2]) and other fyne gold, easy to cary and to

---

1) Merchantys wych cary out thynges necessary to the use of our pepul and bryng in agayn vayn tryfullys and conceytys only for the folysch pastyme and plesure of man. Cardinal Pole in Starkey's Dialogue p. 80.

2) *Rial* oder *ryal* in Nachahmung französischer Stücke hiess nach der Wäh-

have therby wynnyng, by reason it is so reisid into hygh price in other reames, specially in Fraunce.

What shall we say of all straungers, that it is petie so to suffer theym to bryng all such straunge merchaundise in to the hurtyng the comon weale of the reame? To make act by our lawz to bynde theym from so doyng, that wer nother wisdome nor honour to the reame, by owr lawz to rule straungers and putt theym to inconvenyence, to cause theym to reporte yll of the reame. It were more wisdome and honour to ponyssh our own nacion of English merchaunts, that daily stodyeth every oon to distroy the labour and lyvyng of all theyr neighbours. So as they may wynne any riches by byeng all such straunge merchaundize withowt the reame and within the reame, so as they may gete any wynnyng therby, they care not to distroy the welth of the kyng of his lords and of all the holl reame. In exemplum if English men were bownd to a right order, no straungers wer able to hurt England. All straunge merchaunts aught to come and goo free beyng what they list. What defawt aught to be putt to theym, bryngyng owt in to the reame, that myght hurt the comen weale, if English men wold not bye it and receyve it to sell it in the reame elles cowd not hurt.

London to this day hath lyvid at suche a libertie withowt any good order of comen weale, by whose occupieng all England is brought into nede and necessite. The insurreccion on May day[2]) beganne evyn by the inordinat meane of Londoners and not of straungers, but by adventurers and by byers and sellers of all artificialite, wherby all pore handy-

rung von 1465 das neue goldne Nobelstück zu 10 Schilling, *angel* das kleinere Goldstück zu 6 sh. 8 d. Ruding, Annals of the Coinage of Great Britain I, 283.

2) Am 30. April 1517 erhoben sich die Lehrlinge und Gesellen in London gegen Gewinn und Arbeit der Fremden, Italiener, Franzosen, Flanderer, Deutsche, deren Häuser zum Theil zerstört wurden. Alte aufgehobene Statute wurden angerufen, mit den Waffen und dem Galgen eingeschritten. Hall, Chronicle 588; Grafton, Chronicle of London II, 289 ff.; Lord Herbert's Henry VIII. bei Kennet II, 28. Ueber die von allen Gewerben niedergehaltene Arbeiterclasse und deren Erbitterung gegen die Concurrenz der fremden Arbeit L. Brentano, Zur Geschichte der englischen Gewerkvereine S. 79.

craft are brought into nede and necessite. Before May day pore handy craft peple, which that wer wont to kepe shoppes and servaunts and hadd labour and levyng by makyng pyns poynts girdells glovis and all such other thyngs necessary for comon peple, hadd therof sale and profits daily, unto a thirty yere agoo a sorte beganne to occupie to bye and selle alle soche handycraft wares, callid haburdashers, otherwise callid hardware men, that a fourty yere agoo was not four or five shopes in London, wher now every stret is full of theym. Which sellith all fantasies and trifell, in distroyeng all handy craft, wherby many riche men is reson upon that distruction of the pore peple. Which before May day pore peple perceyvid theym self, havyng no lyvyng, and wer bownd prentissis in London, not able to kepe no howsis nor shops, but in allis[1]) sittyng in a pore chamber, workyng all the weke to sell his ware on the Saturday brought it to the haburdasshers to sell, to such as use the sale therof, which wold not giff theym so moche wynnyng for theyr wares to fynde theyr mete and drynk, sayng: they hadd no nede therof, ther shopps lay storydd full of byend see, markyng, than beganne pore artificers to murmur and grudge daily, cursyng for bryngyng such thyngs into the reame. Such haburdashers adventurers shewid to the pore peple, it was not they, that brought so moche in to the reame, but straungers, that brought it over and lay in the citie thorowt the yere and solde it to all haburdashers, as in very deede French men and Flemyngs ever kepith warehowsis and selers at the water side of all such haburdash wares and sellith it to theym at all tymes thorowt the yere. A warehowse with stuffes, estemyd worth a hundred pownde, the werkmanship therof accowntid by it self all the substance, wherof it is made, not worth a hundred shilling, but trifells aforesaid. So the pore artificers in London, being distroyd by occupieng into Flaunders, aswell fullers shermen and all other murmuryd and grudgid, that so putt in to ther heddys straungers was the cause therof, so begane they to rise upon straungers. Which insurection, if the Cardinall[2]) hadd not incontinent subdewid it,

---

1) alleys. 2) Cardinal Wolsey. Ueber sein Einschreiten s. Brewer, Letters and Papers II, p. CCXVI.

the rightwisnes of Godd elles hadd wrought, that suche, as hadd robbid the pore peple in the reme, was likely to have ben robbid theym self. London hath cause to pray to Godd, that it may be reformyd in such wise, that Godd take not vengeaunce upon, that it hath distroyed the holl reame. London is now in condicion, that all the peple therin are merchaunts. So as no man therin can liff with bodily werke to gete his mete, but universally stodieth daily, how to gete lyvyng oon from another by borowyng in wey of byeng and sellyng, covetous and falschode ever werkyng oon to begile another. So many brokers, that sekith bargayns by wey of chevisaunce over long herin to write, how many weys peple in the citie inventith oon to disceyve another, all pore peple, whiche by handycraft can have no lyvyng of necessite fallyng to byeng and sellyng of wynes in cellers and blynd lanes[1], and kepyng alehowsis, sellyng vitall: sowse[2] poddyngs eggs butter chese and other thyngs, over grett mervel to see, how all the citie is soo full of alehowsis, vitallyng howsis, sellers and taverns, full of resort of idull riotous peple, usyng inordinat companyes of hawnts of harlotts, and norishyng such mysorder, that comonly the usage and costance is of owtward famyliarite, every man to desire another to make mery in all such howsis of ryott. For lakke that pore peple hath noo labour and levyng by handy craft, causith all such inordinate rule. If all peple may have labour and levyng well and besyly occupied, shuld cause moche more quietnes in London and thorowt all the reame.

If a wise discrete cowncellor of the kyng by his gracious auctorite and comaundement wold take upon hym to reforme the citie of London, that all comon peple therin myght have labour and levyng in a right order to liff owt of necessite, shuld doo the most hyghest pleasure and help to the spiritualtie of England[3]. That may be, the spirualtie know-

---

1) Sackgassen. 2) to souse, pökeln.
3) Auch Latimer, der London: repent! repent! zuruft, fügt hinzu: And ye that be prelates, look well to your office; for right prelating is busy labouring, and not lording. Works I, 65.

ith not theym self, what shuld be ther helpe, therfor they strive with rigorous means to rule the comonaltie havyng nede to the ware of ther malice and enmite. No thyng can help the spiritualtie, but to help to rule comon peple with charite. Blessid may that cowncellor be, that will soo cowncell theym to suffer the peple to liff in Goddes peace and the kyng in rest and quietnes, and help to support and indyten[1]) hym, that will help all comon peple in England to liff owt of nede and necessite. For dowtles, the very necessite in all peple causith theym to have grudge and envy ageynst the spiritualtie, seeing the welth of the holl reame so distroyed, wherin all comon peple is in such nede, and the spiritualtie in so great welthe causyng all peple to grudge ageynst theym. And so rigorously to handle theym causith theym thynk, the spiritualtie hateth theym, soo engendryng such malice between theym, that wisdom is to help such an amyte for all men to liff togeders in charite. For that entent most wisdome is for the spiritualtie to help all peple to liff owt of necessite. In exemplum, if all peple wer owt of nede, shuld not nede to grudge ageynst the spiritualtie, if they hadd more riches than they have. Wher so having riches and all other peple in povertie, that must nedes prikke theym, and to handle theym with hatrid so rigorously must nedes much more greve theym.

If such a right order may be wrought to help all peple to have labour and levyng quyetly to liff owt of necessite, all the holl reame shuld so liff in peace and quyetnes; and if comon peple myght see the spiritualtie werke besily for that entent, shuld sewerly order in London between the bryngyng in of gold and silver into the reame by straungers for byeng clothes, and the clothmakers, that was wont to receyve it for ther clothes and alwey distributid it thorowt the reame. London between bothe by ther fredom in the citie will never suffer straungers and clothmakers bye and sell togeders for no redy money. But they first bye the clothe of clothmakers, therfore gyvyng both wares and money, and after that so sellith it ageyn for wynnyng, taking therfor of straungers bothe wares and money, that now all mens occupieng is turnyd into wares and

---

1) indite, im Sinne von einladen.

no money. And if all the clothe in England myght be made of trew wolle, sewerly wrought and made in to clothes and sold by record of a staple scale to witnes the sewer makyng therof thorowt all reames, and that dyvers shew dayes of the market may [be]¹) ordenyd fre for all straungers to by clothes of the clothmakers to giff redy money for theym, like as in old tyme, so wold the straungers in all reames putt redy money in to the purses bowgetts²) and casketts to bryng in to England to bye wollen clothe sewrly made and good chepe. To see, what inconvenyence and myschief is wroght for that no staple of clothe is in England, all the Dowch tong, havyng our English wolle at ther pleasure, with Spaynysh wolle doth drape great quantite of cloth, which they sell in hurtyng the sale of English cloth, of which two wolles makith such cloth, that will tak a shynyng glosse with forcibly pressing plesaunt to the jie³), by cause the Spaynysh heyry woll kepe the pressyng, wher English woll of fyne staple will not. And that cloth is thykk and stuffy in the hand to seme fast made clothe, and will not be stretchid owt longer than the length of it self upon no teynters⁴), but rather it will rent in sondry, havyng no staple cannot ratche. So they accownt ther clothes sewerly made to provyde ther own werkmen settyng besyly to werke. And our English clothes of staple woll, which will ratche, they use daily in Andwarpe and other townes to stratch theym upon teynters four or five yards longer in every pece owt only to wyne so moch by the mesure of theym, sellyng theym in to Almayn, but also sclaunderyng English clothes to the pryse of ther clothes, sayng to Almayns, so disceyvid by theym, that English men do falsly make theym, reporting English wolle to be the best wolle, and the wurst makers of clothes and falsist, that can be.

All which myschief and sclaunders is for lakke of a staple and right order not hadd for no comon weale. No man in England never seketh for no comon weale, but all and every for his singler weale. By the wisdome of Adams fall under the sone no mans wisdome attaynyth

---

1) fehlt in der Handschrift.   2) für: budgets.
3) eye.   4) tenter, Spannrahmen.

unto Goddes wisdome, no mans right is meiten nor mesured by Goddes right, that is the standard right of all comon weale. That shuld be the kynges hedd right like as the hadd right of every oon man. What other right hath Godd putt into the hedd of every oon man, but only the right of comon weale of all the membris in his body. What man can say by the office of his mouth, fedyng all the membris in his body, to giff to oon hand more than to another or to oon fynger or to any oon member more than to another, wherby oon to hurt and distroy another, but that alle membris shuld receyve mete togedere to liff owt of necessite etc.

I^a.

Clement Armestrong's Sermons and Declaracions agaynst Popish Ceremonies.

Im fünften Sermon p. 121 findet sich folgende Schilderung der goldenen Zeit, als England noch nicht den Canal beherrschte, der flandrische Markt noch nicht dominierte und fremde Käufer baar bezahlten:

Before the getyng of the narow see and Caleis England lyvyd welthily in itself, whan all peple comonly receyvid ther levynge of Goddes gift with ther labours in right order, before ther was any merchaunte in London, that adventured, before the narow see was goten. Not for that the getyng of the see shuld hurt the reame, but for sufferyng Londoners to cary over it into Flaunders, what they have lustid at their will. Than was no ruyn nor scarsite in the holl reame, whan all peple in London lyvid by ther werkes of artificialite, drapying all fyne scarletts, fyne russetts and other sortes of fyne clothes, whan in London was 720 brode lomes to weif brode clothes. Than was London an artifice, whan all peple therin lyvid by ther werkes of artificialite. Than was never a merchaunt therin, that adventurid over the see. Than was all the holl reame full of welth and plenty of vitalles and money. Than was all the havyn townes in England in welth, occupied with resort of all straungers, that usid to come to theym dayly to bye wollen clothes of the very cloth makers, even at such portes abowt the reame, as all other remes lyeth in course, as all Spaynyardes, Portyngales and other reames toward the south resortid to Hampton, Bristow and other havyns in that parte of the reame, wher to his day the same sorte of clothes most convenyent for theym is yut made ther and now browght to London. And that tyme Lombardes Jennais Italions and Venicions resortid with ther galies, freight with spices and such other comodites, to London to bye alle fyne clothes. And to the havyns toward the est partes in England the Dewch tong resortyd, Esterlynges and all the Loo contreys, standyng in the waters, Holond and Zelond and Flaunders, which than bought our English clothes at portes in England and caried it into Almaigne to the martes beyond Colen, whan never a marte was in all the Loo contreys a thisside the water of the Ryne. Than hadd the merchauntes in the Loo contreys good gayns, that solde English cloth hyghly pricid in Almayn, before they hadd our English wolle at ther wille to drape clothe in the Loo contreys like as they now doo with Spaynysh wolle. And for our English cloth that tyme they brought gold and silver owt of Almaigne, mynted and unmynted. to the portes in England to pay to clothmakers for clothe, which than was myntid in England, whan 7 myntes was in the reame than daily occupied. Than was no such sorte of byers and sellers of all thynges as now is. Clothmakers that tyme recyvid no thynge for English clothe but redy money, gold and silver, which they distributid to all comen peple for wolle and for artificiall werkes of drapery, so as than the holle reame beeng plentifull of money by workes of artificialite, which owt of ther handes for vitalles alwey cam to the handes of fermors, which than occupied all housbondry, and owt of ther handes to the handes of the lordes of the erthe, which than hadde plenty bothe of vitalles and money, more abler that tyme to meynten a greater howshold with more peple more plentuously fedd with ther lande of half the value of the yerly rent than now is. Than was all thynge plenty, whan peple gaff not ther wittes to seke policy by byeng and sellyng to gete riches owt of the comen weale for ther own syngilarite, as now is usid. Than was Stilierde at the ports estwarde lieng toward their parte, whan moo Esterlynges resortid to England than now, by reson our clothes are comonly carid into Flaunders, wher they may bye theym ther better chepe than in England, and sell ther merchandisez ther. Than was the havyns, wher Stiliard place is, daily usid in Hull York Newcastell Boston Lynne and soo to London. Vitalle was so good chepe in London that tyme, whan peple might liff with litle money to make cloth in the citie, wher now vitalle is so dere and scarse, that artificers cannot make artificialite good chepe. Than was not the fourth part of peple in London that now. For so moche as now is all the resort of straungers, and other, that than resortyd to all havyns townes, now resortith to London. Than was no corporacions of no craftes in London nor halles with no constitutions and ordinaunces for no syngularites as now is but the Guyldhall, which was newly recdified a 160 yere agoo[1]. Than was mercers grocers drapers nor such other occupacions namyd. Than was no silke clothe of gold nor of silver nor rich costly apparell worne in the reame, but only lordes such, as for the honour of the reame usid certeyn rich apparell every after his degree and kept it to remayn their heires and successors withowt spoylyng and wastyng the importunat charge of aparell, that now is. And all meane state and comon peple that tyme were no silke. Than all servyng men wer clothid with cloth made in England sadly and honestly, whan they might be knowen from ther lordes and masters, wher now servyng men goth more liker lordes. Than that tyme lordes comonly ware fyne London russettes[2] and other fyne cloth, havyng therof as moch honour and worship that tyme as now in weyryng of silke and cloth of gold. Servauntes that tyme ordinatly apparel was more obedient and redy to doo better service, than now in ther rich apparell absteyn to doo service, now like as than for hurtyng and weryng of ther rayment, ridyng by the wey will now rather giff

---

1) Die Gildhalle der Stadt London wurde bezogen 1411, ein wichtiger Anbau, die Küche, kam hinzu 1501. Cuningham, Handbook of London p. 216.

2) russet, braunrothes Wolltuch.

an ostiler 2 ā lewdly to dresse his horse rather than to doo it hymself for hurtyng his rayment. After that reson all servyng peple thorowt the holle reame are so reisid into highnes of pride disdayn and idulnes by weiryng of such fantasticall apparell, made in straunge reame and brought into England and worne to the hurte of all peple rent to ragges, daily and yerly in kepyng owt the value therof in money, which shulde elles be brought into the reame, wher in old tyme peple ware the cloth, that was made in the reame. Than was many great townes welthely meyntenyd with cloth makyng, which are to see now decayed. Than was wolle caried owt of England into other reamys to selle. In the tyme of Edward the III^{de} no Englishman might cary no merchandise of the staple owt of the reame in payn of forfeture, the 43 yere of Ed. III. p^{o}.[1]). That tyme the werke of housbondry was discernyd to be the cause of comon welth, whan no man shuld make his sone a prentise, but if his father might dispend lande. The comon weale was than considerid. Acte was than made, that English man shuld selle merchaundise to no straungers but for redy money or for part merchandise in hande to lende them naught like as now clothmakers for lakke of sale are fayn to sell ther clothe to Esterlynges, which soone oon runnyth awey with 2 or 3000 L. at a tyme and many such. Before London had recourse over see into Flaunders, all straungers brought gold and silver to all havyn townes in England for all our wollen cloth and for other staple wares for wolle felles lede tynne and hides. Yhe, that amowntid yerly to 300000 L., whan ther was not brought into England of straunge comodites to the value of 100000 L. Whan no silke nor soche quantite of wynes nor artificiall straunge fantasies was brought into the reame that now is. So that in old tyme whan all the merchaundises of the holl reame amountid litle above 300000 L., bowt by straungers for money brought into the reame, and by straungers caried owt of the reame. Than

---

1) Jan. 25. 1369—Jan. 24. 1370. Das Statut 43 Edw. III. c. 1 zog wegen des Krieges den in Calais errichteten Stapel zurück und bezeichnete eine Anzahl Seeplätze in England, Wales und Irland, Westminster eingeschlossen, als Stapelorte. Vgl. Macpherson, Annals of Commerce 1, 576.

was brought yerly into reame abowt 200000 L. in gold and silver, and the reame never had lossis nother of shipps nor of merchandises upon the see, nor by lendyng of merchandisez to straungers. And than before Londoners adventurid into Flaunders, whan all havyn townes was occupied with straungers, than hadd gret nomber of comen peple welthy levyng by ther portage cravage¹) and cariages of merchandisez in all havyn townes by resort of straungers, wher they usid and ostid²), alwey spent ther money in the reame. In London that tyme was no merchantes inhabited nor kept no howsis but the Esterlynges. All merchants of the south partes came with ther galies caricks or shipps to London to discarge by a certayn tyme and bye ther clothes to charge ageyn and depart. Before Londoners caried English clothes into Flaunders and made martes in the Loo contreys, merchantes of the south partes hadd no occasion nor cause to occupie into Flaunders and in the Loo contreys. Whan all the marte was holden in Almayn and toward Venys and other staple townes in thos partes, caried ther merchandise to the martes in Almayn by lande. So that than all the merchantes of the south partes hadd no occasion nother to inhabite and lye in England, but very few, that than hadd licence to sell and retaile vitaile wynes and spices. In example that tyme of that act of licence the first yere of Richard the II³) ther was no craft or name of grocers in London. The name of oon John Donote or such other name that tyme a straunger, that sold spices in London, was beried in the westende of the chirche in the Frere Augustyn⁴) in London by his name upon the stone to this day to see callid

---

1) cravage, wenn von *to crave*, Angebot; aus den Wörterbüchern jedoch nicht nachweisbar.
2) used and hosted, verkehrten und einkehrten.
3) Juni 22. 1377—Juni 21. 1378. Das Statut 1 Ric. II. c. 1. 2 gestattete fremden Handelsleuten in England Wolle, Tuch, Metall und die anderen Hauptartikel des Landes frei ein- und zu verkaufen, vgl. Macpherson Annals of Commerce I, 587.
4) Die Kirche der Austin Friars in Broad Street Ward, City, wurde nach Unterdrückung der Klöster 1550 von Edward VI. der protestantischen Gemeinde der Holländer übergeben, die sie heute noch besitzen.

piperarius, for a peperer by his occupacion and no grocer. To understande all ther names of craftes hath ben corporatid within a 140 yere[1]) by reson that London syns that tyme occupied into Flaunders caryeng owt of the reame all such merchandisez into Flaunders, which all straunge merchauntes before that tyme bought in all havyn townes within the reame, than all havyn townes by processe of tyme decayed in conclusion utterly distroyd as is to see. So as after London hadd goten all the recourse of the holl riche comodites to passe by ther handes carieng it owt of England into Flaunders, than begane London to brede and encrease merchaunt adventurers, of which the mercers, that tyme callid lynyn drapers, were the first in London, that to bye lynnyn clothe, callid that tyme whit ware, they to bye it at the first hande in the Loo contreys in Flaunders, after the narow see was English began first to be adventurers. etc. etc. etc.

I[b].
A lettre to my maister I can not tell from whom.

Please it your Mastership to consider, wher I have bene your servaunt in my mynd this three yers takyng tyme labour and payne to help to sett forth the knoledge of the right order of comen weale of all peple in the realme, to the entent that ye shuld help the kyng to sett it up to be mynestrid in exemplum to all other realmes. And right sory have I been, that your mastership wolde never inwardly see and know the image of the kyng upbering upon his shulders the chirch of Crist in his hevynly manhode, which is signyfied in an ordinary seale of his hedde office. Non other right order can be of a comen weale but by

---

1) Von den zwölf grossen, den sog. Livery companies, besitzen nur die Fishmongers eine Incorporationscharte, die bis auf Eduard I. zurückgeht. Stubbs, Constitutional History of England III, 574.

a like ordinaunce mynestrid in erth like as in hevyn. Your mastership knowith, all my pore desire hath been over all thynges, that ye shulde help all peple to liff owt of necessite and scarsite, yong and old. seke and holle, that therby the kyng may first opteyn and wyn the myndes and hertes of all his comen peple. For though it be thought an acte impossible to doo, the order therof is made in such a forme, that lakkyth but the mynestery to doo it in deed. All peple, that is able to werke, by ther werkes shal be kept owt of nede and ete ther own mete to deserve it before they etc it, and all peple not able to werke somes of money shal be gatherid in the realme to kepe theym owt of necessite, above 400,000 L. every yere. And the kyng of his own tresore shall pay no peny, but shall be gatherid of such, as shal be gladd to pay it for ther own avauntage. All my pore mynde hath been with charite to shew, how all peple shuld be kept owt of necessite. Your Mastership knowith well, I never therfore axid any wordly promocion nor rewarde. And wher I delyvered two bokes to your Mastership before Alhalloutide last past, in which apperith somewhat of the distruction of the comen weale of the realme and somwhat of the remedy, and wher I profered my servyce to your Mastership to be in your howse with the help of a faire writer to sett forthe the knowledge of all thynges, apperteynyng to the right order of comen weale, whan your mastershipp provysed, I shuld so doo. And for not so doyng I desired of yow three daies before Cristymes to have the said two bokes, that I myght have wreton in theym many moo thynges apperteynyng to the right order of comen weale, which ye yitt know not. And the last yere in the meane tyme, whan I occupied my mynde abowt such thynges, I have been robbid by a false felow, whome I toke to be my servaunt and putt hym in speciall trust to oversee the werkmanshipp of a wode sale, which I bought of the busshopp of Wynchester beyend Wyndsore, and delyvered to hym at dyvers tymes the some of 363 L. to pay all the charges therof, wheras after the Cristymes I callid hym sodenly to make his accownt. And so he hath made a boke of his accownt, wherin he confessith hym self, he hath receyvid the seid 363 L. and chargith hymself with all the stuff, which he hath made therwith. But of the stuff he hath solde as moch as amowntith to the some of 251 and more unknowen to me, and therwith hath bought a wode sale in the name of two other men in the contrey pertyners with hym and his cowncellers to werke that falsehode. And wher now that goodes beeng owt of his handes and so sodenly callid to his accownt, lurkith and hidith hymself in the howse of oon John Grymes in London in Seynt Lawrence parish¹) and dare not be forth comyng, which Grymes kepith hym in his howse and mayntenyth hym to withhold the seid 200 L. So am I robbid of my goodes and cannot get²) the partie. Wherfor if ye wilbe my good maister, I may have a easy short remedy withowt any trouble in the law. So as it may please your mastership to send for the seid Grymes, commandyng him to bryng forth the seid Weders, to be savely kept unto such tyme he shall make aunswere to alle thynges he hath chargid hymself with in his seid boke of accownt to show, wher my goodes is, and to restore it ageyn, as moche as by an indifferent auditor can be provid, he hathe so falsely inbesselid. Or ellis, if the seid Grymes wille not bryng forth the seid Weders, to doo that, whiche is rightfull accordyng to conscience, it may please your mastership to compell the seid Grymes soo to doo as a man withowt honestie to meynten such a false felow with owt shame. Your seid servaunt thus beeng quyetid in his mynd shall writ you the clere knoledge, how to sett up Cristes chirch, whiche was never yitt sett up nor Cristes faith never mynesterid by no generall forme syns Cristes ascension, and shall show your mastership the mynestracion of the order of comen weale and the offices therof, and what is the kynges levyng on his part, and the levyng of the prest on his part; how the levyng of the busshop and decon risith owt of the werkes of the sole in the chirch inwardly, that is the tithes, and the levyng of the kyng risith owt of the werkes of the owtwarde bodyes of the peple, that is the rentes of the erthe. And to shew, what the offices are of the busshop and decon by ther offices

---

1) In der Nähe von Cheapside.
2) Original: getin.

doyng to receyve ther levyng; in example, if the office of decons had been mynestrid in England, the comen weale of the reame shuld never have been distroyd. Your Mastershipp shall see the resons, how to begyne first to sett up a right order of comen [weale][1], and what reasons to be declared to the peple in consideracion therof. A right order of comen weale can never be made by no mens wisdome of afterwitt, but by Goddes wisdome of forwitt with charite. As God was before the devile, grace before syne, lyve before dethe, the image of the kyng must be lyvely by mynestery, that all the solles of peple in his holl realme must be in cure and knoledge in his hedd office, and that mynestery must be by the office of dekons, that no unlawfull peple be sufferd to wander owt of cure in the holl realme. Your seid servaunt is redy to shew yow, how to begyn this order incontynently for you to doo that dute, wherby to wyne the gretist love and favour of all the comons of the holl reame above all the councellors of the kyng[2] that ever was.

II.

How the Comen People may be set to worke an Order of a Comen Welth.

All inordynate lyvyng among people in any realme is only under sufferaunce of the kyng, for any kyng in governyng his people under any other law, than only Godes law, can never fulfyll Godes wyll in his office, nor all the kynges, that ever was or shal be on the erth, can never make better lawes, than God hath made, nor in no wyse any kyng ought not to awgmente theire owne wordely power, but only in executyng Godes ordynary powre. And that every kyng within his realme ought to con-

1) fehlt im Original.
2) Da sicherlich an Thomas Cromwell gerichtet, zu einer Zeit, als dieser schon Mitglied der Privy Council war, also schwerlich vor 1531. Cromwell wurde im October 1534 Master of the Rolls und im Jahre 1535 Vicegerent und Generalvicar.

syder, what comodytie God hath plantyd within the precyncte of his domynyon and acordyng as God by his ordynary law gevith the encrease theroff, so ought all kynges and mynysters to receave it of the gyft of God, that is he shulde se his people set to worke ·the saide gyfte acordyng to the nature or qualitie of the gyft, and that the workers theroff, to receave there lyvyng by theire labonres, and that the thyng to have the increase, so ought all kynges to have all proffytes or increase within there realmes, the which is over and above, that all theire subiectes hath no nede.

For as a kyng, clamyng his kyngdome by mans law, is but a subiect to that law, havyng but a certayne stepende apoynted to hym by that law, where as by Godes law he is lorde of all within his domynyon [1], as it apearyth playnly in Samvell the VII chapter [2]. And to bryng it passe that all people within his realme to be brought owte of nede fyrst must be to set all people to worke in order of a comen welth, and that is to understande, that there may not be any man sufferde to lyve owte of right order, which right order I do understande thus, that the whole bodie of a realme is a mysticall bodie, wherof the kynges maiestie is hed, and as his maiestie is the hedd of this mysticall bodye [3], so are all degrees of people within this realme the bodie and members of the same hed, and lyke as it is a greffe to the hed of any partyculer body to have any member sore or sycke of his particuler body, even so ought it to be a greffe to the generall and mystycall hedd to have any member sycke sore in the mystycall body, ether to suffer any member of the saide mysticall body to lyve owte of order of a comen welth of the saide bodye. Now whether it be for a comon welth of a bodye to mayntayne strange members to the disturbanse of the whole bodie, as lawyers, which are

---

1) Offenbar in Bezug auf das Doppelkönigthum, wie es mit dem Kirchensupremat Heinrichs VIII. seit 1529 zur Thatsache wurde.

2) Gemeint ist 2. Samuel. cap. 7.

3) In ähnlicher Scholastik über Volk und Regierung Cardinal Pole in Starkey's Dialogue p. 46: the one may, as me semyth, ryght wel be comparyd to the body, and the other to the soule.

mayntenors of stryffe and debate betwen members of the mysticall body of this realme, and also merchauntes byers and sellers of the comodities of this realme, which of plentye do make scarcitie and cawse members to be in nede and in necessitie, also whether it may be thought or imagined, that one member of a body can be more holyer than an other, ye or nay I thynke not. Then owght there not one freare monke chanon nor other clokyde ipocrit to be sufferde within the mysticall bodye of a realme, for trueth it is, there is no trew member in a mystycall bodye but hathe an office to laboure, which utturley they refuse to do, but say: they owght only to pray, so that they take to them the office of the mowth in the mysticall body, which office had an[1]) end, when owre Savioure Christ came, for he saide: owre prayer must be in spirite and truth[2]), which is in hart and mynde and not in the mowthes of men, as was in the tyme of the olde law. For althoughe there is in a mysticall body of a kyng thes degres: man, kyng and prest, yit is there no sectes of such fayned holynes but such, which ar rebukyd in Mathew the XXIII[3]), which are worthy to be cast owte of a mystycall bodye. And that all true members of a mystycall bodye shulde worke and laboure in degre and order, that they are called to, and none to be sufferde to do any thyng, but only that, which myght be to the welthe of the whole body and members of the same in order as here after shall folow. To understande even, as God hath ordeynyd in the hedd of every man the cownselers that is to saye: the iyes, the nose, mouth and eares to be associate with the kyng, which is reason, and that they altogether shulde studie only for the profite of theire whole bodie, owte of which bodie theire welth doth spryng, so owght the kynges maiestie with his most honerable cownsell to studie the welth of the comens, theire bodie and members, and that the armes of his mystycall body be strechyd fourth in to all this realme, as is shewide in the office of the mynesters, to se that the handes and fyngers of this mysticall body do worke those workes

---

1) and, Handschrift.   2) Evang. Joh. 4, 24.
3) Evang Matth. 23, 13–17.

which shulde kepe the bodie in helth and welth, which is, that husbondrye may be sett up in such sort, that there may be plentie of meate and drynke to fede the bodie of this realme, and that vitall may be so plentyfull, that men of artificiall ocupacions may kepe servauntes to worke those necessaries good chepe, which is nedfull to be had for the whole bodie of the realme, and by settyng people to worke the erth with plowes and then to sett up artificialitie, when vitall is good chepe, and that men may have servauntes good chepe and for lytyll money, than shall all people be set to worke, which now begg, steale, robbe and morder for lacke of lyvyng.

Whan all sortes of people be set to worke by an ordynary order, than shall folow a quyet and a plentyfull tyme. For as the decay of this realme is chiefly by layng downe the plowes and not makyng of clothes in good townes, so must it be inhawnsede to welth, fyrst by settyng up husbondrye, and that clothes to be made in goode townes, which may very easely be done. For the settyng up of plowes may thus be don, as I thynke, yf it wolde please owre most gracious kyng by the advice of his most godly cowncelors to sende fourth commyssions to all shires in Englande, and commawnde, that in every village within this realme the most awncient people therin to be broughte before the commyssioners, and that the commyssioners there declare openly to the people, that it is the wyll and pleasure of owre most gracious kyng to know, what grownde lyeth ydle and not occupiede, the which hath byn occupiede in tyme past, and that it is the wyll and pleasure of the kynges maiestie and his most honorable cownsell to se such grownde put to such use agayne only for that intent, that his naturall borne subiectes shulde not lyve in such mysery, as of late they have done, and that only for theire sakes his maiestie by the godly advice of his cowncelors entende the welfare of his subiectes in that behalfe, and that all such people within any vyllage to take an othe to declare treuly, what grownde hath byn tylde, which now is laide to pasture, the which is hurte to the inhabytawnce there¹). And although in many lordshipes within this realme

---

1) Die unter Eduard VI. am 1. Juni 1548 zur Ausführung der Statute Hein-

the tenawntes wolde not or dare not shewe trewth, it shall be no matter gretly to passe an act the first tyme, so that all such grownde, which shalbe openly declarid to be usid contrary to the welth and comodytie of the comynaltie to be imployede to husbondry. So shall the comen people be the workers of the kynges pleasure in this matter, and the kynges maiestie may commawnde all lordes, which hath theire landes in theire owne handes, to set up plowes themselves, and all fermores, which hath takyn leases of growndes, to tyll the erth themselves and set up plowes or elles to give up theire lease to the lorde, and that the lorde to sett in such, which shall tyll the erth, as is afore saide. For comenly in all places riche fermers be the kepers of such grownde, that is laide to pasture, therfore they may wel be commawndyd to make plowes and to set men to worke theire erth, which theye have in ferme. So in all quarters within this realme I thynke there wyl be 30000 plowes set to worke therth mo than now do, so at the least I thynke 30000 men servauntes shal be set to worke, which now lyvith in myserable case. Some men thynke, it wyll set an hondrede thousande comen people to worke within this realme. Now, yf there may be an hondrede thousand set to worke by hosbondry, what a decaye is it to this realme not to worke the erth. wherby thees people myght be set to laboure for the welthe of the rest of the people within this realme.

I have harde say, the tyme shall come, and that by olde prophecies, that Englande shal be paradise, which I thynke veryly cannot be untyll such tyme, that people be set owt of all evell order, the which they now are in, and that people be first sett to laboure the erth to make plentye of vitale, that artifycers may be wyllyng to take the resydew of the kynges subiectes to worke artyficiall workes, the whiche shulde be nedfull for the whole realme, besydes also that it may be commawnded, that no clothe to be made but only in the good townes within this realme, which townes shulde shortly prospere agayne, as they have of

---

richs VII. und Heinrichs VIII. ertheilten Instructionen, abgedruckt in Strype's Ecclesiastical Memorials II, 2. 359, lauten in der That sehr ähnlich.

long tyme decaide. Also I thynke it were good, that the kynges most honerable cownsell, yf they wyll reforme the realme, to make an act of Parlement or other wyse a decre in the Starre chamber, that all cities and townes within this realme to make ordynawnce for the welth of the saide cities and townes, and that than the inhabytaunce of all cities and townes to have in commawndement, that they do make and ordeyne among them, that no thyng be brought by any of the kynges subiectes frome any strange place beyonde the see, the which may be wrought in any partie of the kynges domynyon[1]), upon payne of forfit of body and goodes to the kynges highnes, and that all workers of artificialitie to be set to worke as well strangers as Englyshmen, and that because the good workmanship of all artificialitie is most comenly sene in strangers and that is by reason of exercisyng themselves in workyng of althynges in maner the which is occupied in Englande, so that all Englyshe men hath cleane loste all corage to studie for all such feates, and that because we have so many marchantes, the which hath no other lyvyng but only to by all maner of artyficiall workes, wroughte by artyficers in the parties beyonde the see, and to bryng than hether in to this realme, so that the whole realme is stuffed with fances and tryfulles, that in maner the rychese of the whole realme lyeth in strange merchandyse, the which byers and sellers bryngyth in to the realme other wyse to call them marchauntes, the which dothe as moche as in them liethe to dystroye the welthe of the whole realme. Also it wolde be decreed, that what stranger so ever he warr that brought any maner of workes of artificialitie in to this realme at any tyme, that they may costome[2]) it and do with it what they wolde and as they now do and to carne it or way or gane at theire pleasure, so that no inhabitaunt within this realme do by it upon pane to forfit it and theire bodie and goodes to be at the kynges pleasure excepte such thynges, which cannot be wrought within this realme, which decre shall cawse no stryffe nor variance betwene prynce and prynce in

---

1) They marchaunt must be prohybytyd to bryng in any such thyngys wych may be made by the dylygence of our owne men. Cardinal Pole in Starkey's Dialogue p. 174.

2) *to custome*, verzollen.

that it shall not be agenst no contracte made in any tretie of peace, so that ether subiectes as marchantes may carie what comoditie they lyst and whether they lyst. For I thynke, it is not agenst no tretie of peace, that any citie or towne shu..de devise for theire comen welth, thoughe per adventure it be agenst the tretic of peace, that the kynges maiestie or his cownsell shulde make any law to inhibite, that no comoditie of any foren realme shulde be brought in to this realme, within whome the kynges hyghnes hath concludyd any such tretise. And yf it shall be thought nedfull at any tyme, that some certayne workes of artyficialytic to be bowght of any stranger, yit shall it be bought by the consentes of the comynaltie, the which I shall speke of more at large, when I speke of the artifycers in London.

What a losse is it to se all bodyly workes of comen people dystroyde, which shulde not only helpe to kepe all people owte of idolnes to lyve in a right order, but also shulde increase the welth of the whole realme, as for an example: yf all wulles ware drapede in the realme, the workes of the people shulde be moch more worth than the wull, so that yf there ware but halfe the wull that now is, and that it shulde be drapede, it wolde be more worth to the realme, than now is all the wull and the shepe that berith it.

So to set as many people to worke all such erth as is before spokyn of, and the residew to be sett to worke artificiall workes, which now is wrought beyonde the see, so shall the grete nomber of people within the whole realme be set to worke savyng those, which shall seme to be sycke and sore etc, the which I wyll shew in the provision for them, how theye also shalbe providyd for and how the most parte of them shall or at the least may laboure for theire owne meate, which shall ease all comen people of theire grete charge, which theye now are at in gevyng to them theire almost. And although this my rude wrytyng semes not to shew clerely the order of artificers, yit, as I have saide, all the comen people within this realme may very well be set to worke by husbondrye and artificialitie. And of artyficialitie shall I shew more at large by it selfe here after in the order of artificers[1]).

---

1) Die offenbar unvollendete Abhandlung komnt hierauf nicht zurück.

Where as there was a commawndement came downe from the kynges most honorable cownsell 10 or 12 wekes past to all prynters, that they shulde prynt no maner of new thyng, onlesse it be sene of those, which know what is necessary to be comen among the kynges subiectes, the which is nedfull to be observyde[1]). But I thynke, it ware good, that a commawndment shulde come to all such, the whiche do prynte or cawse to be pryntyde any maner of Englishe boke grete or small, that they nor none for theym prynte any maner of thynges in Englysh withowte the kynges domynyon upon payne of the kynges dyspleasure and to forfite the same. For although that bokes pryntyde beyonde the see 8 or 10 yeres paste[2]) hath done myche good to the comen people of this realme for the knoledge of such thynges, which the papistes did what they colde to hyde, yit I thynke for as moch as it is the kynges most gracious wyll, that any thyng, which may do good to his lovyng subiectes, shulde be set fourthe here within this realme. This consyderide I thynke, it ware goode none to be sufferde to prynt any thyng withowt this realme, ye, and also that all haberdashers to be commawndyd not once to bryng any maner of primers[3]) frome any place beyonde the see nor no other boke to sell here within this realme, which be or shalbe here after pryntyde beyonde the see and brought frome thence by strangers or other. And in shorte tyme it shulde well be sene, that the pryntyng shalbe a comodious syence and shulde set many of the kynges subiectes to worke, wherby many shulde wex rich, which now are in maner but beggers. And also it shall sease the uncharitable and inhordynate fasshones, which now is dayly usid emonges prynters and booke sellers, as whan any man hath pryntede any thyng, that is vendyble, streghte waye one or other wyll prynt the same in disspite of hym, that first did print it, and wyll

---

1) Leider sind die Protokolle des Geheimen Raths aus der Mitte der dreissiger Jahre nicht vorhanden.

2) Eine Anspielung auf die Uebersetzung des Neuen Testaments, welche William Tyndal 1526 in Worms und 1534 in Antwerpen drucken liess.

3) Fiebel und Katechismus in einer Gestalt, wie denn auch die ersten anglikanischen Liturgien sich in dieser Form hervorwagten.

say: what prevelege hast thou, I will prynt any thyng for myne owne advauntage, so that there is nother honestie nor goode order among them, the which is grete petie.

And all thynges owte of goode order goith to wrake and comyth to naught. Where as yf there were goode order among them, there myght be many of the kynges subiectes be set to worke such thynges, which now men are dryvyn of necessitie to have strangers to worke, the which strangers here within this realme dystroye moch vitale abhomynably in suche wyse, that I thynke God is hyely dyspleasid therwith, but in gydyng the people in order of a comen welthe I shall showe my mynde, how that all such unsaciable persons may be gydyd in good order. Also as I understande the byble shal be pryntyde beyonde the see[1]), the which myght be as well done here within this realme as in any other realme, and as goode cheape and as quyckly done. And as I thinke it ware a good policie for governers and rulers of a realme alway to studie, which way to set all comen people to laboures to kepe theire frowarde myndes well occupiede and not to suffer such thynges to be wrought owte of this realme, the which may easely be wrought within the realme. The cownsell of Frawnce hath ordeynyde that no man shall pay costome for pryntede bokes, and that becawse men shulde rather have such thynges pryntede there, the which shulde sett many comen people to worke, wherby they wex ryche and have money enoughe to pay theire dewtie money to theire kyng, and whan any man is myndyd to have any white

---

[1]) Bezieht sich auf die englische Bibel Coverdale's, welche seit 1535 wiederholt in Antwerpen abgedruckt ward. Auch die erste Ausgabe, „set forth with the Kinges most gracyous lycence . . . published in London by Grafton and E. Whitchurch" 1537 ist dort veranstaltet, cf. H. Stevens in Caxton Celebration Catalogue 1877 p. 122. Nach Lord Herbert, Life and Reign of Henry VIII. in Kennet, Complete History of England II, 213 ertheilte der König durch Cromwell das Privilegium an R. Grafton, „who pretending the wont of good paper here got our King's and Francis's license to print it at Paris both in Latin and English", was den vorhandenen Exemplaren nicht entspricht. Im Allgemeinen standen Druck und Einband aller Bücher unter Protection, seitdem durch 25 Henr. VIII. c. 15 ($153^3/_4$) die einst durch 1 Ric. III. c. 9 ($148^3/_4$) gestattete freie Einfuhr aufgehoben wurde.

paper unpryntede, he paith grete costome therfore, becawse the comen people lesyth theire laboure of it. And as for paper myght be made as well in Englonde as in Fraunce, so that people myght be set to worke in makyng the paper as in pryntyng of it. And yf rulers wolde ayede suche, as hathe myndes to prove such profitable feates, men wolde gladly spende[1]) such, as God hath sent them in the proffe of such matters, which myght hapely turne gretly to the welth of this realme. As yf there be any, that wolde take upon them to prynte the whole byble in dyvers sortes, and such one to have a prevelege, that none shall prynt the same nor none other but he, and he to be bownde to bylde a paper myll or twayne and to mayntayne the same. And I thynke, 2 paper mylles wolde make as moche paper, as wolde serve all the prynters in Englonde, the which shulde be a grete comoditie to this realme.

III.

How to reforme the Realme in settyng them to worke and to restore Tillage.

Our sovereigne lorde the king of Englonde, firste considering, in what welth the body of his realme was abought 27 yeres passed[2]), and secundly perceyvyng, by what meanes it is now dekeyed and made feble week and power[3]), by reason that the labours and lyving of all common people, members in the body of his realme, hath been distroyed, causing necessite and scarsite of mete and drinke, clothing and money, thirdly his grace and his lordes hade now nede to perceyve and knowe the remedy how to restore the body of his realme to a more welth then ever

---

1) vielleicht verschrieben für speede.

2) Heinrich VIII. trat die Regierung an April 21. 1509, so dass die Denkschrift den Jahren 1535 oder 1536 angehört, in denen sich die Regierung ernstlich mit wirthschaftlichen Fragen befasste.

3) poor.

it was in, as moche as Godd hath not otherwise ordenyd it. therfor the king and his lordes hath nede to mynyster right ordre of comon weale, or elles they muste nedys distroy their owne weale by the very ordenaunce of God, for they are upholden and borne upon the body. Yf they wil be riche, they muste firste see all comon people have richis, that out therof must rise their richis and all the people be out of nede. A riche welthy body of a realme makith a riche welthy king being the hedd therof, and a pore feble weke body of a realme muste nedys make a pore feble weeke king. Our sovereign lorde the king of Englonde cannot gather habundaunce of golde and silver out of the handes of comon people in the body of his realme without they have it.

Therfor his grace muste firste percyve and knowe, what plenty of golde and silver is in the realme, and that golde and silver may be brought out of other realme and contreys into Englonde as moche yerly, as the king thinkith to gather out of the handes of the comon people, or elles muste nedis make scarsite of money in so moche, as no gold nor silver growith in Englonde, but that shuld be brought out of other contreys into England for the rich commodities growing therin, which Godd yerly gevith to all the common people to worke for the welth of the body of the realme.

The holl welth of the body of the realme risith out of the labours and workes of the common people. Therfor to make due serche: who distroyith the labours and workes of common people muste nedes distroy their lyvinge in as moche, as Godd ordenyd not erthyly men to ete but yf they worke, as Paule saith: he that will not worke that he ete not[1], never ordenyd erthly men to ete but he labour and worke. lyke as the firste erthly man was put into the image of the lorde Gode, as it is wretyn, that he shuld worke, before God gave hym to ete his giftes of grace, in example that he and all men shuld worke in that image of our Lorde, that saith in Eccles. XXIIII[2]: who worketh in me shal not

---

1) Thessal. II, 3. 10.
2) Gemeint ist Ecclesiastes 2, 24—26.

do syne, that is to understande: who workith in me to receyve my giftes of grace thorow faithe, shall not do syne. The highnes of faith is in state of grace over syne and judiciall law and under grace. In example, yf we lyve not in highnes of faith, whether cane we receyve grace? Paule saith: we be saved by grace thorow faith [1], and in an other place he saith: all thinges of which is not of faith is syne [2]; ergo yf we lyve out of faith in workes of syne under judiciall lawe, not justified from workes of syne by faith without workes of the lawe, how cane we receyve grace? And yf we have not grace, what avaylith all lernyng and knowledg, though we have knowledg of all thinges both good and yll, yf we have not grace to doo the only good and forsake the ill, what causith us to doo ill but syne, that workith in us for lake of grace and before lake of faithe? Ergo then muste we all lyve in grace, yf we entende to receyve the giftes of grace, which giftes we have nede to pray to Gode to give us and that we may worke to receyve theim to encrese the common wealth of the body of Englonde to uphold and maynteyn the welth of our sovereigne. Geff hyme mete, yf he be able to worke. He that workith not, ete his owne mete agenste right of faith, for that is syne.

Considering ther ar but two workes for the comon weale of the body of the realme: workes of husbandry to encrese plentie of vitalles, and the workes of artificialite to encrese plentie of money, the moste parte of the common people muste be sett to husbandry to worke for their bodyly lyving, for as moche as our bodyly lyving is more nedfull then our clothing. For that entent it may please the king to sende his commyssioners into every shere howse within the body of his realme to serche thorow every borow towne and vilage to have parfit knowledg, how many plowes land and how many plowes hath been occupied and how many may be occupied in the hole realme to till the erth by workes of husbandry to encresse plentie of mete and drinke for our bodyly lyving, and upon that serche and knowleg the kinges gracious mynde towerdes the common weale of all his people may be proclaymed in all

---

1) Rom. 3, 24. 25.   2) Rom. 14, 23.

his market townes, how his gracious entent and will is, that as many plowes as hath been occupied in his holl realme in old tyme shal be occupied ageyne, wherby the moste parte of his comon people shall have labours and lyvinge to lyve out of necessite and scarsite as many as ar able to worke. Our gracious king thus doing shall firste reyne the hartes and myndes of all his common people members in the body of his realme. After the moste parte of his common people so sett to the workes of husbandry to encresse plentie of vitalles, the other lesse parte of his people to be set to the workes of artificialite to make clothing and to make all other thinges nedfull and necessary, wherby to encresse plentie of money, wherwith to by ther bodyly lyving. So shall all the workers of husbandry have plentye of money for their vitalles of the workes of artificialite, and so shall the one parte of the people worke for meate and drinke and that other parte for money.

Wheras now so grete nombre of idull people ar in Englonde besyde all such that workith husbandry havyng no workes or artificialite to gete money wherwith to by there meat and drinke of the workes of husbandry. And all the same idull people havyng lyff in theym must nedys have lyving. Ergo yf they be[1]) workes of artificialite gete no money, wherewith to gete their lyving, muste nedes bege or stele their lyvinge from them, that workith husbandry, or otherwise by craftie meanes of beying and sellyng or by policy to study howe of plentie to make scarsite for their singulare weale to distroy the common weale, that is the wisdome of this worlde. For yf all people be not sett to labour and worke to lyve out of necessite, elles muste they nedys sike[2]) their lyvinge by their wisedome and policye. In example to see how alle the workes of syne and wykednes is wrought in suche people as of necessite ar sufferid to seke theire owne lyvinge, every man like as his liste. Every pore manes sone borne in labour is suffered to be a merchaunt, bier and seller, which never workith to help his neybores nor never stodith for a comon weale but for his owne singulare weale. Alle suche cane never lyff in charite, for charite never seketh his owne thinges.

---

1) by.   2) seek.

All workes of artyficialite as well makers of wollen clothes and all other thinges muste nedes dwell in market townes to worke for money, for God hath ordenyd, that gold and silver shulde be brought out of other contreys into Englonde for wollen clothes and for other commodities, which God gevith yerly to the realme. otherwise cane be no plentie of money in the realme but brought in for our riche commodities value for value. So long as our owne English merchauntes ar sufferid to cary our wollen clothes out of the realme to sell in other contreys and for theym bring in no gold nor silver into the realme, never shall be no plentie of money but riche merchauntes and merchaundizes and pore king and lordes and pore commons. Therfore all clothe makers and other artificers muste dwell to gethers in market townes like as in olde tyme, and the high prices of all sortes of woles in the realme muste be mynyshed to the low price agayne as in olde tyme. For that entent the felowship of clothers and stapellers muste be called before the kinges grace and his honorable counseill to shew by the recordes of the staple bokes, what prices all sortes of woles bought and sold in Englonde but 124 yeres[1]) passed, and theruppon to charge alle stapellers and clothmakers to pay no higher price for woles now like as in old tyme. That is no new invencion for people to murmur or to grudg, yf the king restore his common people members in the body of his realme to the same welth, that they were in olde tyme. What one man shal be agenste that acte of the common weale, a thousand comon people shall hold with the king agenste that wiked man for the mynyshing of all sortes of woles to the half prices, lyke as they were in old tyme. Yt shall cause the pasturers of shepe to open their closiers[2]) and suffer the more erth to be wrought by workes of husbandry to encrese the more plentie of vitales in the holl realme, that clothmakers and all other artificers may kepe their howsholdes good chepe and geve lesse wages to all artificers to make Inglishe clothes and all other thinges good chepe.

1) Würde von 1536 aus gerechnet etwa mit dem Ende der Regierung Heinrichs IV., 1413, zusammentreffen.

2) enclosures.

Wherupon it may please our gracious king of Englond to make a staple of all wollen clothes in London and that all clothe makers with their artificers dwell to gethers in market townes like as in old tyme, and that every market towne of clothe making have a common seale and every wollen clothe made within the presinct and libertie and fredome of the towne to recourde the trew making of all wollen clothes so sealed with the sealles of the townes, wherin they be made, theruppon to be brought to the kinges staple of wollen clothe in London ther to be sealed with the kinges seale of his staple to recorde all the wollen clothes made in Englond, bought and sold by way of the kinges staple, having the staple seale, shal be openly knowen to be trewe made clothes, whersoever they be bought and sold. So shall all Englishe clothers never be slaundered in no other realmes and contries for false making, like as merchaunte adventurers in London hath caused fauls clothes to be made in Englonde for low prices to trucke and barter theym for merchaundizes and slayte wares in other contris for forcyng for their owne falshod nor for the slander and dishonor of the realme. And under the pretence of the same slander merchauntes in Anwarpe and other contrys and townes in the Loo contries hath and doth use to streche Englishe clothes upon tayntors five or six yerdes longer in every clothe[1] and so sell theym unto the Almaynes, which muste nedes shrynk ageyn. And the Almayns complaynyng of that falshod, the merchauntes of the Low contryes, which doth so falsily, excusith themself saying: Englishe wole is the beste, but the clothes draped therof ar falsely made, which saying helpeth the sale of their owne contrey clothes made with Englishe wolles and Spaynyshe wolles, which will not suffer to be streched. And their untrue saying slaunderith the sale of Englishe clothes for lake that their true making of theym is not recordyd by a staple seale.

A staple of wollen cloth in London shal be the moste notable thing for the honor and profite of Englond that ever was, by reasone of good

---

[1] If his cloth be seventeen yards long, he will set him on a rack, and stretch him out with ropes, and rack him till the sinews shrink again, while he hath brought him to twenty seven yards, Latimer, Works 1, 138.

chepe wolles shall cause grete nombre of common people to have labours and lyvinge to make good chepe clothes of true making, which shall cause all strangers to bring plentie of gold and silver into Englonde yerly to bye moche better chepe clothes at the kinges staple in London, then cane be made in other contreys. And all clothes, that strangers shal bye of the very clothmakers at the kinges staple, shall pay redy money for theym, gold and silver, like in olde tyme. And at the kinges staple to have a chaunge kepte, wherby all sortes of strange gold and silver mynted and unmynted shal be serchid assaied and valued at rather higher prices in Englonde then in other contries, to cause all strangers to bring the more plentie of gold and silver yerly into the realme for theire own[1]) advauntage. In that maner wyse gold and silver shal be brought into Englonde for all wollen clothes solde at the kinges staple in London within the realme.

But then muste an ordre be made, that Englishe merchaunte adventurers in London shall pay as moche custome as strangers doth pay for all wollen clothes caried out of the realme to sell at the martes in the Loo contries, for by reason that merchaunte adventurers pay almoste 4 s. lesse custome of every cloth then strangers. Therfor so longe as all strangers may by clothes of Englisshe merchauntes at the martes in Flanders better chepe then in Englonde and save 4 s. in every clothe for the custome, will not by clothes in Englonde. Therfor the policy to cause all strangers to bring plentie of gold and silver yerly into Englonde to bye clothe, such an ordre muste be hadd, that clothes muste be solde at the kinges staple muche better chepe and trulyer made then in other contreys, and that all strangers and Englishe merchauntes pay like custome to cary all wollen clothes out of the realme, and that shall profite the king every yere more then 16000 L. in his custome and shall cause all strangers by their comyng into Englond to bye wollen clothes at the kinges staple to spende above 20000 marckes[2]) of their owne money in the realme for their expences costes and charges. Wheras

---

1) Handschrift: owe.
2) Die Mark nach alter englischer Rechnung zu 13 sh. 4 d.

Englishe merchauntes by carrying wollen clothes out of Englond to the martes in the Loo contreis to sele spendith of their owne money above 20000 marckes every yere for the expences costes and charges. By that reason they have made other contries riche and Englonde pore. Wherfore yf a right ordre may be hade to cause all strangers to bye their clothes in Englond at the kinges staple, then shall they bring gold and silver into Englonde and pay yt to clothmakers above the value of a 28000 L. every yere, and then shall clothe makers cary the same money into all market townes of cloth making in the hole realme and shall distribut it to the artyfycers, which shall pay it to fermours and husbondmen of the contrey for wolles mete and drinke.

By whose handes the same money shall come to the handes of the king and his lordes of the erthe, by that meanes to have plenty of money not to have nede to seke wisedome and policy by actes of parliament to gether money out of the handes of common people of that litle store, which is within the realme, but all way to have plenty of money, which shal be yerly brought into Englonde out of other realmes. And for the subsidew of that 28000 poundes a yere, which the king shulde have, yf it ware retorned in wares and merchaundizes, as it hath been to the distruccion of the holl realme, his grace shall have 12000 L. every yere for the scale of his staple, which shal be more profitable to his grace, and so grete plentie of gold and silver brought into Englonde by his staple shal be more profitable to the hole realme, considering the riche commodities, which God of his grace gevith yerly to Englond, how ther is yerly caried out of the realme abought the value of a 600000 poundes. And therfor is not 10000 L. in gold and silver brought yerly in Englonde more then is caried oute by owne meane and other, in example what scarsite of money is alwayes in the realme. And by reason of gret abundaunce of strange merchaundyses and wares brought yerly into Englonde hath not only causid scarsite of money, but hath distroyed all handycraftes, wherby gret nombre of common people shuld have workes to gete money to pay for their mete and drinke, which of very necessite muste lyf idelly and begg and stele or seke their lyving by suche faulse meanes, as it is to see, how people cannot lyve in right order one with an other, because the king being the hede of his lordes knyghttes and squiers, which ar his harmes[1]) handes and fyngers, doo not mynystre to all common people bodyly members suche giftes of grace, as God yerly gevith to theym, which they shuld worke for the common weale of the hole realme.

All people in England lyvith comonly evyn as they lyste with workes of syne and myschif to gete singler richis one frome an other having no drede of Gode, but only dreding the actuall paynes and ponyshment of the law, howsoever the wiked people workith myschief to distroy one an other, wherby to dystroy the comon weale of the hole realme. What so ever they doo, no remedy is in Englonde, yf ther be no acte of parliament made to the contrary, and whan any playnyth of the distruccion of the welth of comon people is brought afore the king and his lordes in the hedd howse. Therfor cane they make no acte nor good order for the welth of the common people, but remyttyth all causes to pase[2]) by the wisedome content will and agrement of theym, which ar in the common howse, thinking that suche, as ar in the common howse, shuld specially entende the welth of all common people, the kinges bodyly members. Who woll serch may prove, whether suche sortes ar not in the common howse, which hath distroyed the welth of the king and his lordes and common pepole gettyng every yere above 200000 poundes out of the common weale into their syngler weale, whether ther be not fermors in the common howse, which hath gotten 6 or 7 or 10, 12 or 14 farmes of the king and his lordes, and by ther leases ar made lordes of theire lande and by that reason withholdith the lordes erthe frome the workes of the common people. And whether the enclosiers of pastures for shepe and graciers and regraters of corne and catalles ar not in the common howse and merchauntes byers and sellers, which gettyth their richis out of the common weale, alway studying by their policy of plenty of all thinges to make scarsitie, so as by their meanes common people ar brought into nede and necessite to worke syne and

---

1) arms. 2) pass.

myschiff. And whether lawers ar not of the common howse, which gettyth their richis rysyng out of the workes of syne and myscheff of the common people for robbyng and stellyng richis one frome an other and for disceyving and begilling on a nother and for stryf variaunce and debate on agenste a nother[1]. In example whether the richis, that merchauntes beyers and sellers and lawers gettith of the common people yerly, risith not out of their necessite and scarsite vexacion tribulacion angwise and payne. Ergo whether thos sortes in the common howse may well content and agre, that all common people shuld lyve out of suche workes of syne and myschif, out of which they gete all their richis. And yf the king and his lordes in the hedd howse wold mynyster the riche giftes of grace to the comon people, which God gevith theym yerly to worke for the common weale of the hole realme, they in the common howse, which hath and doth distroy the common weale, cannot suffer no acte passe for the common weale, but they muste nedes distroy their owne singuler weale.

Therfor the king and his lordes of the erth hath nede to ordeyn. that the common weale of the hole realme may by his mynysters to be mynysterd in all market townes, wherin all wollen clothes ar wrought and made, for therin the common weale restith. And by that reason the king and his lordes shall never more be trobeled with no workes of actes of parliament for the common weale, but to the governors and rewlers of his riche townes, which shall have gold and silver brought out of all other contries for our wolles and wollen clothes etc. value for value. Therfor all the gold and silver brought into Englonde by strangers shal be in market townes by clothmakers paied for wages to their artificers, which with the same money shall bye vitalles of husbande men and fermers in all contreys in the realme and by their handes the same money shall come to the handes of the king and his lordes and so shall gold and silver encresse yerly in Englonde and make the holl body of

---

[1] Lawyers, whose covetousness hath almost devoured England, Latimer, Works I, 318. Bycause he for hys lucur deludyth bothe partys and prolongyth the controversy by hys crafty wytt. Cardinal Pole in Starkey's Dialogue p. 191.

the realme riche, and so shall the king and his lordes be riche like as in old tyme to have no nede to stody, how to gader money out of that litle quantitie of money, which is in the handes of the commons, in the realme to make scarsite.

    All lordes were riche in olde tyme, which kept welthy howsholdes and bilded substanciall howses not having the riches now able to doo suche actes by reason of the riche commodities. which God giveth yerly by all the common people to worke for the common weale of all the holl realme, which common weale is now distroyed by a few pore mens childern suffered to be merchauntes beyers and sellers having all the holl commodities in the realme in their handes to occupie like as they liste. Therfor Engloude cane never be made a riche realme but by the meanes of a staple of wollen clothe, that all strangers may bring gold and silver into the realme, wherwith to by clothes of the very clothmakers. And that all sortes of wolles in Englond may be bought and solde for half price now like as they were but 60 yeres paste shall cause the more nombre of common people to drape clothes and to worke theym so substancially and truly by the recorde of every towne seale, wher they are made, and theruppon to be brought to the kinges staple to be seald with the staple seale to recorde their true making in all contries, whersoever they shalbe bought and sold, though any strangers in other contries falsely hurte theym by straynyng or otherwise, yf they have the seale of the kinges staple, shall wittenyse their true making. whan they were bought at the kinges staple. And if it can be provide¹), that any Englishe men by clothes at the kinges staple and worke any fansed²) with theym in Englonde, before they be caried out of the realme, wherby the wittenyse of the seale of the kinges staple shuld be slandered, that all such shuld be ponyshed in example. The very cause, wherof all strangers shal be glade to bring plentie of gold and silver into Englonde to bey clothes at the kinges staple, shal be by reason, that woles shal be so grete chepe, and that shall cause the more erth to be tilled by workes of husbandry and make vitalles good chepe.

    1) proved.   2) falschood.

So as all clothmakers may kepe howsholdes for lesse charge and pay the lesse money for wages and for all workes belonging to clothmaking which muste nedes cause all wollen clothes to be so grete chepe and suerly wrought, that all strangers shal be glade to bring plentie of gold and silver out of all contries into Englonde daily to bye theym at the kinges staple to be kept in a convenyent place in London, callyd Ledyn Hall[1]), which is a goodly howse for that entente, and therin to kepe a chaunge appertenyng to the kinges mynte in the Tower, that all gold and silver brought into the realm by strangers unmynted and all strange coyns, which ar not curraunt for clothmakers to pay to common people in the realme, shal be chaunged into Englishe coynes by the keper of the chaunge at the kinges precyd[2]) at the mooste value to cause all strangers to bring plentie of gold and silver into the realme, to understand how that the mynyshing of the pricys of money in Englonde hath alway caused grete quantite of money to be caried out of the realme by our owne Englishe merchauntes moste of all other. For when all barred plakkes[3]) wer firste disabullid and secundly all Romans grottes and pence of 2 ₰ and after that dandy prattes[4]), which were caried out of Englonde unto the martes in the Loo contreys by Englishe merchauntes, some

---

1) Leadenhall war ursprünglich ein grosses Manor-House, seit 1445 vorzüglich als Kornspeicher der City, aber auch als Packhaus für Wolle benutzt mit einer Waage für dieselbe, so noch unter Elisabeth in Stow's Tagen, Cuningham, Handbook of London p. 282.

2) precept.

3) *Plack*, eine alte schottische Kupfermünze, *barred*, weil auf dem Revers das schräge St. Andreas Kreuz mit einer Krone darüber und je einer Fleur de lis zur Seite abgebildet ist. Die Vorderseite zeigt die Diestel mit der Krone, wie J. M. Thompson, Assistant Keeper of Manuscripts im Britischen Museum, gütigst mittheilt. Auch in Holland kamen Placken als Kleinmünze des Gulden vor, Koppmann, Hanserecesse IV, 574. $14^{00}/_{01}$.

4) Sind *Romans grottes*, Groten, Groschen, etwa grobe Reichsmünzen, die vortheilhaft gegen das kleine englische Silbergeld eingeschmuggelt wurden? *Dandy prattes*, bei denen vielleicht an Danzig zu denken wäre, cursierten in England als sehr kleine Silberstücke, Notiz in Notes and Queries 20. April 1878.

one caried over a busshell at a marte; and when galy halfpens[1]) not weying 4 of theym oon peny, yet were they better then on peny worth of slite merchaundizes as wynes and silkes, ones every yere piste agenste the walles and torne to ragges, better to have plentie of gold and silver in the realm then plentie of merchauntes and merchandizes. Galy halfpence was a necessary money for all pore peple, though they, whiche brought theim into the realme, hade grete profite by theym. Therfore never banyshe no gold nor silver out of the realme, but all people have knowledg, at what price to receyve it of strangers to the moste value. And he that kepith the chaung at the kinges staple to cary all strange gold and silver mynted and unmynted at the kinges mynte in the Tower of London. And that no man be sured to hier nor ferme the kinges mynte for no singuler weale to refuse the receyving of strange gold and silver, which shuld encresse riches for the common weale.

The kinges grace for diverse consideracions muste take the fredome of London into his handes to make his staple at Ledyn Hall free for all strangers, wher as to this day strangers and clothmakers cannot bye and sell togetheres in London but by the meanes of a freman of London, by whome all strangers beyeth clothes at the seconde hande, therfor bringeth all maner of merchandizes to London to barter for clothes and no money, and likewise Londoners barteryth merchaundizes for clothes with the clothers and litle money. In the charter of London is wretyn, how the fredome shall not be takyn away for no fence of any one man but for the offence of the holl citie agenste the common weale of the holl realme, as it is not convenyent to suffer on man to distroy an holl occupacion or an occupacion to distroy a holl citie nor one citie to distroy the common weale of a holl realme. Therfor the king hath nede

---

[1]) *Galey halfpennies*, nach Ruding, Annals of the Coinage of Great Britain I, 250. 254. 271, Kleinmünze aus schlechtem Metall, schottischen und ausländischen Gepräges, die, schon unter Heinrich IV., Heinrich V. und Heinrich VI. verboten, während Heinrich's VIII. Regierung noch nicht ausgetrieben war. Nach Stow, Survey of London 137 wurde sie mit den Galeeren (galley) von Genua und Venedig eingeführt, Notes and Queeries 27. April, 1. Juni 1878.

to take the fredome of the citie into his handes, unto[1]) his grace hath reformed diverse causes for the common weale of the holl realme. The salve muste worke the remedy in London, wher the sore is furste[2]). The kinges staple in Ledyn Hall muste be made free for all strangers therin to bye all wollen clothes of the very cloth makers and pay theym redy money not to be interrupte ne letted by no fredome of the citie. And yf a fewe citizens now lyving thinke their bying and selling of wollen clothes shal be distroyed by that meanes, all riche men being agyde[3], ar out of nede and yong men may set upe draping of fyne wollen clothes like as afore tyme, and therby gete their lyving truly withowt any crafte or policy. Secondly ther muste be a somme of money ordenyd in London so moche as shall vitall the holl citie in itself to have no nede of no vitalles in the contrey. The cause of all grasiers and regraters of corne and catalles and of all maulte men hath been onely for that London hath not made provycion to vitall itself. so as never shal be vitalles in London plentie for pore people to drape fyne wollen clothes nor to make all workes of artificialite good chepe before London vitall itself lyke as it was vitalled in old tyme. Ther is money inough in London for that purpose, though nother the king nor no man lyving geve nor lende no peny therto like as it shal be shewed, how whan tyme shall require and all the ordre of mynysters and officers in the citie ordenyd to make all provisions of vitalles for the citie. On notable provicion shal be to encrese plentie of vitalles in the holl realme by reasone that the citie of London and all other cities and market townes of clothmaking in Englonde shall have stokes of money every in itself to make provision to vitall itself, that all artificiall people therin may make all thinges grete chepe. And by that reason having stokkes of money shall bye their vitales alway of the pore husbondmen, which riche fermors graciers and

1) statt until.

2) Der Antrag den Freibrief Londons zu widerrufen ist gegen die grossen Gilden (companies) gerichtet, die alle commerciellen und politischen Privilegien der Stadt an sich gebracht hatten.

3) vielleicht verschrieben statt agreede.

regratours²) bieth grete chepe of pore men for nede and sell it ageyne derely to all artificers in market townes. For all biers and sellers of vitalles sekith daily of plentie to make derth and scarsite. Therfor the workes of artificialite must have stokes of money in every market towne to by vitalles of the pore workers of husbandry the oon sorte to helpe the other, and so distroy all such sortes as byeth and sellith vitalles for their owne singularite.

The remedy to encresse all Englonde with plentie of vitalles shal be by reason of the stokkes of money in all cities and townes of clothmaking in the realme, so as the king and his lordes shall not nede to troble theymself to make no actes of parliament, which cane never prevayle, seing how no acte for the common weale cane passe these sortes in the common howse, which gettith their riches from the commonaltie to their owne singularite. And for the common weale will not distroy their owne singuler weale, all merchauntes byers and sellers in London or elles wher ar commonly pore mens sones naturall borne to labour for their lyving, which after they be bounde prentises to be merchauntes, all their labour stody and policy is be bying and selling to gete singler richis frome the communaltie and never workith to gete their lyving nother by workes of husbandry nor artificialite, but lyveth by other menes workes and of naught risith to grete richis, entending no thing elles but only to gete richis, which knowith no common weale. For as moche all other stodye is onely for their owne singler weale, merchauntes in London may be excused by their ingnorauncy, though they have distroied the plentie of vitalles and money in the holl realme, they knowe not how nor by what meanes, but lyvith after the common course of merchauntes, gett richis how and by what meanes they force not in their conscience, not dreding the rightwise judgment of God, but for dred of the law they axe counseill of lawers, what richis they cane gete, whether

---

2) Gegen dieselben ländlichen und städtischen Speculanten eifert Latimer: we have landlords, nay, steplords I might say, that are become *graziers*; and burgesses are become *regraters:* and some farmers will *regrate* and buy up all the corn etc. Works I, 279.

they may hold it and kepe it by the law that no acte be to the contrary for fere of losyng therof. In example to se, whether all merchauntes in experience doo not so lyve only under the lawe without faith after a staple of wollen cloth is set upe in London. All and¹) so lyvith without faith cannot have grace to lyve in the will of mercy of God, that is the new testement, for by grace all men ar justified and savyd thorow faith. All thinge, what is not of faith, is syne.

All wollen clothes made in all townes of clothmaking in Englonde, before they be brought to the kinges staple, muste have the seale of the towne wher they ar made, and at the enseyling therof the clothmaker to pay one peny for the weving and one peny for the fulling and one peny for the dying, that is a grott of every cloth, which the clothmaker shall stope in his handes in paying the wever fuller sherman and dier, and that grote to be putt to the common stokk of the towne to vitall the pore artificers besyde other money daily reisid for the same pores. By suche reason of all stokkes shall ryse and encresse in market townes of clothmaking in a shorte tyme and riche clothers may lende their money for that purpose in meane tyme and have it ageyne.

Suerly the common weale of Englonde muste rise out of the workes of the common people. The workes of husbandry encressith plentie of vitalles and the workes of artificialite encressith plenty of money. What sorte distroieth the workes of common people distroieth Goddes workes and causith necessite, for God gevith no mete to common people, but by their workes the workes of common people shall encresse Englonde 400000 marckes every yere in golde and silver more then hath been. In example to consider how ther is caried out of Englonde in woles wollen clothes tynne leede²) and hyddes etc. abought the value of 600000 poun-

---

1) idiomatisch für *who*.   2) Von den drei alten Handelsartikeln Englands singt Crowley 1550: This realm hath three commodites,
    Wool, tin and lead,
    Which being wrought within the realm,
    Each man might get his bread.
Vgl. Starkey's Dialogue p. 173 und p. CLXXIV.

des every yere in gold and silver yerly more then is caried out daily by on meanes or other. And wheras merchaundizes is now brought into Englond yerly to the value of a 400000 marckes more then was in old tyme, which myght be spared or made within the realme not only to save so moch money spent out of the realme, but also to sete common people daily to worke in a right ordre of the common weale to kepe theym out of idelnes frome working syne and myschif, ther is now brought out of other contreys into Englonde to the value of a 100000 poundes of lynnyn cloth every yere. In example if every parishe in Englonde spente but 40 s. in shertes and smokkes and other lynnyn besyde that that is made with in the realme, grete nombre of yonge maydens and women may be set to spyne lynnyn cloth, which lyvith idully in hordome and bawdery, marvelyng to see the foly, how Inglishe merchauntes spendith in Flaunders a 100000 marckes a yere for lynnyn cloth, and they have banysshid Englishe wollen clothes and ther will suffer non to be bought. And the wynes now browght into Englonde to the value of 100000 marckes more then in old tyme may be spared, which is spent emonges unchristie people and oons every yere pyssed agenst the walles. And the silke which is brought into Englonde to the value of 100000 marckes now, which was not in olde tyme, may be spared, and so grete nombre of common people may be set to worke so moche the more wollen clothe to clothe all people lyke as in old tyme, when no silke [was][1] worne nor usyd. And ther is 100000 marckes in value of artificiall thinges made in other contreys brought into Englonde yerly, which may be made by worke of common people within the realme as well as without. This value of 100000 marckes in merchaundizes brought into the realme yerly to make such ordre, that it shal be yerly made within the realme.

And that all strangers may bring gold and silver into the realme to by wollen clothes at the kinges staple will cause theym to bring 27 or 28000 L. at the leste to cary theym out of the realme paying no more custome then Englishe men. And to bye theym so grete chepe shall cause all strangers to resourte to Englonde now ageyne like as in old

---

1) fehlt in der Handschrift.

tyme. And considering how the staple of woles by reasone of the good chepe wolles shall bring a 500000 L. in gold and silver into Englond yerly that more then 200000 L. by meane of bothe stapelles now accompt the resydew of the value of 600000 L. yerly incressed of the commodities of Englonde, ether muste Englishe merchauntes[1], what they cary out of the realme, ether muste they bring into the realme the value theroff in substanciall nedfull merchandizes as odde[2] alame madder and woll oyle and such other thinges for draping of wollen clothes, and all manner of spices and iron pyche tere wex bowstavis coper lattyn wyer and all other thinges which is neadfull for the common weale of the realme, which Godd hath ordenyd in other contreys and not in Englond and what Englishe merchauntes cariethe out of Englonde to more value then all such nedfull merchaundises must therfore bring gold and silver, for as moch as they shall no more bring into the realme suche thinges as may be sparid or made within the realme to the value of 400000 marckes by yere, by such an ordre Englonde by Goddes grace may shortely be made a riche realme. One reason is wherby merchauntes in London hath gretly distroyed the common weale of the holl realme by receyvyng such thinges of strangers as hath been to the distruction of the common people, for no strangers could hurte Englond by bringing in any merchaundises into the realme, yf no English merchauntes wold by it and receyve it to the distruction of the realm. Esterlynges of Spruse and of other parties in the Est contrey hath been profitable merchauntes for the realme in olde tyme, before they toke Coloners into their Haunce.

---

1) hier fehlt in der Handschrift ein Verbum wie *custom*.
2) statt *woad*.